Let's Speak Ilokano

Let's Speak Ilokano

PRECY ESPIRITU

University of Hawaii Press
HONOLULU

96   6 5 4

Library of Congress Cataloging in Publication Data

Espiritu, Precy, 1937–
  Let's speak Ilokano.

  English and Iloko.
  Includes index.
    1.   Iloko language—Text-books for foreign
speakers—English.   I.   Title.
PL5752.E86   1984   499'.21   84–16015
ISBN 0-8248-0822-3

Lovingly dedicated to
Laurie
and to my brothers,
Emmanuel,
Vitaliano, *and*
Efren

Contents

Acknowledgments

I express my heartfelt gratitude to the following people and institutions for their contributions to this project:

To Lawrence A. Reid, Department of Linguistics, University of Hawaii at Manoa, for his generous help in editing and proofing the various drafts of the manuscript;

To my colleagues, John Mayer, Josie Clausen, Janet Lagat, and Irma Peña for much useful feedback;

To Rosie Sagucio and Marilyn Macugay for their skillful typing of the various drafts of the manuscript;

To the Department of Education of Hawaii for the initial funding of this project;

To the Department of Indo-Pacific Languages for assisting in various ways in the different stages of preparation of this textbook;

And above all to all my students who continue to provide me with inspiration in my teaching and writing.

Introduction

Let's Speak Ilokano is designed to enable students to attain fluency in speaking Ilokano in a limited number of social situations. In order to achieve this, emphasis has been placed upon interaction between students, rather than between student and teacher, as students usually find it easier to communicate with their classmates than with their teacher. The role of the teacher in this method is primarily that of resource person. He or she is there to provide a model for pronunciation, to give an Ilokano word as soon as a student asks for it, to provide explanation for a grammatical point, and to encourage and stimulate interaction between students.

The lessons have been designed for students. Instructions are directed to students. Even drills, wherever possible, have been constructed to maximize interaction between students.

A language learning class should be fun. To help create that element, a variety of games, communication activities, and dramatic situations form integral parts of each lesson. These activities are designed to reinforce old and new material and to elicit spontaneous conversation. The teacher should include new games, new ways of playing old games, and variations on the dramatic situations in lessons. New situations in which the students can exploit the language they have already learned also should be provided.

No matter how realistically a dialog is acted out, it must be remembered that it is an act, that the language classroom situation and much of the dialog is contrived, and to that extent artificial, even though the language itself may be natural. The teacher who is interested in helping his students speak Ilokano will therefore involve the students in social situations, such as a party, ball game, or visit to a restaurant or home where Ilokano is spoken. Students should be required to use Ilokano in these situations with the teacher always available as a resource person. Student-created plays may be used to provide repetition of vocabulary and structure and writing practice. Skits are good vehicles for learning intonation and for developing naturalness of speech.

Let's Speak Ilokano contains fifteen lessons, providing enough material for a full year of learning Ilokano. The teacher should not feel bound to a schedule of one lesson every week or one lesson every two weeks. He should proceed at the students' pace, always being aware of the need to keep interaction brisk.

In formulating the dialog used in this text, the overriding principle has been to provide natural speech, using language which is normal and appropriate to the context of interaction. In order to do this it often has been necessary to introduce a variety of grammatical constructions or verb forms within a single dialog.

Each new grammatical point is discussed in the Grammatical Notes and a variety of exercises is provided to help students understand and use these forms. The teacher should make sure that the students grasp the usage of each new grammatical point, and should be ready to supplement the drills and activities as necessary to meet the students' needs.

Slower students should be paired with faster students at least half of the time. This gives the slower student the opportunity to learn from his peer, and provides the faster student with a sense of importance in being able to help someone else learn what he has learned. Frequent interchange of partners of varying abilities will help the faster student to obtain the stimulation needed to continue his own learning.

In devising the methodology used in this text, I have been inspired by a number of stimulating works on the teaching of foreign language, all of which are oriented toward the development of communicative competence in the target language. I am particularly indebted to Richard A. Via's *English in Three Acts* (Honolulu: The University of Hawaii Press, 1976) for my basic approach. His concept of using drama as a vehicle for achieving competence in a foreign language has been used in Ilokano classes at the University of Hawaii for some time with excellent results. The Dialog Modification and Role-Playing sections of each lesson in this text are adapted from ideas developed by Richard Via.

Another source from which I gleaned ideas was the concept of the teacher as resource person, developed by Charles Curran in his Community Language Learning approach, a method of self-learning in which the students are in complete control of what to say, to whom to say it, and when to say it, with the teacher telling them how to say it. Gertrude Moskowitz's *Caring and Sharing in the Foreign Language Class: a Sourcebook on Humanistic Techniques* (Rowley, Massachusetts: Newbury House Publisher, Inc. 1978) also has been valuable in stimulating ideas for ways of developing communication between students in the classroom. Ideas for additional communication activities and language learning games have come from sources too numerous to be mentioned here. I wish to express my thanks to each of them.

Notes To The Teacher

1.   A NOTE ON SPELLING.   There is considerable inconsistency in the way Ilokano words are spelled. The few available dictionaries offer little assistance. Primary areas of inconsistency are in the spelling of words with u or o, and in the use of y and w. An attempt has been made to be consistent in spelling in this text, but the spelling given sometimes is not the same as that which is often used. The principles followed are:

     a.   The O vowel is used in native Ilokano words only in the last syllable of the word, *aglúto* (to cook), *agdalos* (to clean up). If there is a pronoun attached, the spelling will remain the same, *aglútoka* (you cook), *agdaloskami* (we clean up). If there is a verbal suffix, however, *o* will change to *u, lutuen* (to cook), *dalusan* (to clean). Spanish and English loan words are generally spelled as they are pronounced even if *o* occurs in a syllable which is not final, *nalóko* (bad), *bolpen* (ballpoint pen).

     b.   The words *lutuen* (to cook) and *pilien* (to chose) provide the pattern for vowel sequences in which u and i are the first vowels. Notice that there is no *w* in the first word, and no *y* in the second word.

     c.   Although *y* is not added between a final *i* and a suffix, it is added between a prefix ending in *i* and a vowel-initial root, *iyeg* (to bring), *iyáwat* (to pass), *iyúper* (to soak).

     d.   Accent marks usually are not used in written Ilokano, but since the position of stress in a word is significant, *ápo* (term of respect), *apo* (grandchild), accent marks are used in the text so students will learn how to pronounce words correctly. When stress occurs on certain syllables, the vowel is pronounced long. In this text long vowels are marked with an accent since these are the most prominent vowels. A word which does not have an accent mark is stressed on the final syllable, but the vowel is short.

2.   THE DIALOG.   Every lesson centers around the dialog. Understanding the meaning of the dialog is an absolute prerequisite for successfully learning the dialog. Attempts at presenting the dialog

before the students fully understand what it is supposed to mean can only lead to frustration and loss of interest.

In order to find out what the dialog is all about, the student must study it. This should be given in the form of an assignment to be done at home or at the language laboratory, in order to leave as much class time as possible for interaction between students. The student should compare the words in the dialog to the literal translations provided. He should then try to construct a natural sentence in English that he thinks says what the Ilokano is saying. After completing the free translation, he should refer to Appendix One, and compare what he has written to the free translation given there. The two translations need not be identical, but they should be consistent in meaning.

Assuming that the students know the semantic content, the teacher is then ready to present the dialog. This procedure has several purposes. Its primary purpose is to associate Ilokano forms with their meanings. The student hears the words and how they are pronounced and begins the process of learning them. This procedure is therefore a listening exercise. It is also a writing exercise. The student reinforces his or her mental image of the words by learning to write them correctly.

The presentation procedure is as follows.

a. Instruct the students to listen and concentrate (preferably with eyes closed) while you read the dialog through once. Be sure that your pronunciation and intonation are clear, but maintain a natural pace in speaking. Try using different voice tones for the different speakers.

b. Instruct the students to write the dialog as it is dictated to them. (Students should write on alternate lines to leave room for corrections to their copy.) Dictate the dialog clearly and slowly, repeating each word or grammatical phrase at least twice.

c. Read the dialog through once more slowly while the students correct their copies.

d. Ask one or more of the students to read the entire dialog from his own script.

e. Ask the students to take turns in dictating the dialog to you or to another student line by line while you or another student write it on the board. Repeat each line before writing it. Do not forget to add the accent marks as you read the line over. The students should correct any error in the sentence on their scripts before moving on to the next sentence.

f.   Say each word and its translation aloud, underlining each word as you go along. The students can join in this oral translation. Translate the word or phrase as a whole. Do not attempt to give literal meanings for grammatical words like *nga* or *ni* or verbal affixes. The student will learn the significance of the grammatical markers when they study the grammar sections.

3.   LEARNING THE DIALOG.   Once the student has studied the dialog and participated in the presentation procedure, he should already be fairly familiar with both its form and its meaning. It is now essential for him to complete the memorization of the dialog. (By this time he should already have internalized some, if not most of it.) Although learning a foreign language requires a great deal of memorization, this need not be a painful or difficult process. Done within the context of a simulated play or game, memorization can be relatively easy.

A variety of procedures for learning the dialog, nearly all of which require student interaction are suggested in the text. In Lesson One, teaching the teacher, the roles of student and teacher are reversed. The teacher's real (and simulated) memory failures, and other learning difficulties place him on a par with the students. The students prompt him until the teacher has actually learned the dialog. His constant repetitions provide models of correct pronunciation for the students.

4.   ROLE-PLAYING.   This section is designed to reinforce learning the dialog and to provide an emotional ingredient which is present in most real-life communicative situations. In the early stages of learning the language, some students may feel shy about acting in roles assigned to them. Most students soon overcome this initial embarrassment and are able to enjoy it.

Creative drama techniques can be used to elicit spontaneity while providing listening practice and review of vocabulary and structure. For example, the teacher can instruct the class in Ilokano to, "Be a tall statue, a frightened dog, an offended old woman, a cranky little boy", depending on the vocabulary learned. Such activity develops spontaneous movement and expression without students having to worry about producing language at the same time. The activity is good preparation for other role-playing students will be required to do, either in acting out lesson dialogs, or in performing student-created plays.

5. VOCABULARY. This section contains words that need to be learned in order to do the Dialog Variations and the Exercises. Once again, learning can be fun. Games like "Vocabulary Horse Racing Sweepstakes"* provide a competitive stimulus to learn words, and to produce them instantly on demand. Variations of the game can be used to teach conjugations of verbs and other appropriate skills as well. The teacher can take the class outdoors to name objects in the natural environment or to perform actions and give the Ilokano equivalent for them. English borrowings regularly used by Ilokanos are included. The student should be encouraged to speak Ilokano even if he cannot recall the correct Ilokano word. Substituting an English word on the spur of the moment to enable a communicative event to take place is far preferable to not speaking until the correct word can be found. Often by the time the word is found the opportunity to speak has passed. The teacher always should be ready to provide an Ilokano word or phrase as soon as it is requested, rather than telling the student to look it up in the glossary or to try to work it out for himself.

6. DIALOG MODIFICATIONS. There are two sections in this activity. The first provides sets of stimuli for modifying specific parts of the dialog. These are indicated by numbers appearing above each dialog section, e.g., 1, 2, 3, 4, to divide the dialog into a set of mini-dialogs. The substitution of an item in one of these sections usually requires a corresponding change in the answer. The modifications are contextualized substitution drills. The second dialog modification section requires modification of the whole dialog, for example, where the social status of the participants is changed, requiring new pronouns and terms of address throughout the dialog.

Dialogs often end with a question or require further conversation to be complete. Students should be trained to complete the dialog by making culturally appropriate exchanges. For example, the exchange in a dialog fraught with conflict is considerably different from one which is a casual conversation.

---

*The basic format of this game was introduced to the author by Stephen Egesdal, a former student of Ilokano.

Dialog modification requires student interaction. The teacher should always be available to assist the students in giving correct forms and keeping the communication alive. Partial modification is often best accomplished in small groups of not more than four students. Full dialog modification can also be done in small groups or can be attempted impromptu in front of the class with the students acting out their parts.

7.   QUESTION AND ANSWER.   The primary purpose of this section is to give the students practice in the use of structures which are associated with information questions and their answers. It also will test comprehension of dialog. This is a good section to use as a home assignment. Students can study the questions and their meanings (translations are provided in Appendix One), and think of various ways in which the questions can be answered consistent with dialog content. In class students then may take turns asking and answering the questions with partners. Students should be encouraged to ask thought-provoking questions relating to their experiences in relation to the dialog.

8.   GRAMMAR NOTES.   Learning to speak a language is not dependent upon learning the grammar of a language. All children learn to speak their native language without a word of grammatical explanation. However, the teacher should be prepared to explain grammatical detail when a student asks why something is said a certain way. The grammar notes have been written to assist in making these explanations. The terminology used is not as important as the principles of word, phrase, and sentence construction. The teacher should remember that grammatical notes are written in the context of the dialog. They do not attempt to describe all, or even a major part of the grammar of Ilokano.

Every lesson contains a set of written exercises to reinforce learning grammatical points discussed in the notes. Students should be encouraged to refer to the grammar notes when they do the grammatical exercises.

Sufficient cultural notes have been included to enable the student to understand cultural points in the dialogs.

9.   COMMUNICATION ACTIVITIES.   These activities provide contexts for the practice of vocabulary and structures learned in the lesson. Some of these activities require the student to do independent language elicitation, in order to gain skills which can help him

or her learn the language independent of the classroom. The teacher should encourage students to utilize language mastered in previous lessons.

10.   WRITING PRACTICE.   Writing exercises are provided for most lessons. They reinforce what was learned in the lessons and are a good means to detect and remedy errors. Besides developing creativity in the language, writing exercises also force the student to focus his attention on the structures of the language.

11.   LISTENING PRACTICE.   Each of the lessons in this text has been prepared in a way intended to enhance not only the verbal skills of the student but also his aural skills. Oral fluency does not necessarily imply good aural comprehension. Training the ear is as important as training the tongue; because effective communication can only occur when both tongue and ear are trained. The listening exercises should be considered as important as the rest of the lesson.

Lesson One

I. DIALOG: Getting to Know You

Study the following dialog. Try to understand the meaning of each sentence by referring to the literal translations of the words on the right.

1

			naimbag	good
1. A:	Naimbag a bigatmo, Mis.		a	linker
2. B:	Naimbag a bigatmo, met.		bigatmo	morning-your
	2		Mis	Miss
			met	also
3. A:	Ania ti náganmo, Mis?		ania	what
4. B:	Luz ti náganko.		náganmo	name-your
5. A:	Ania ti apelyídom?		náganko	name-my
			apelyídom	surname-your
6. B:	Ulep ti apelyídok.		apelyídok	surname-my
7. A:	Aya? Ay, Ulep met ti		apelyído	surname
	apelyído ni Nánangko!		aya	is-that-so
			ay	oh
8. B:	Ay, kasta? Ania met ti		nánangko	mother-my
	náganmo?		kasta	like that

II. TRANSLATING THE DIALOG

Write a free translation of the dialog (i.e., a translation in natural English). Do it in pencil, and then check it against the translation in Appendix One. Make whatever corrections are necessary.

A:_____

B:_____

A:_____

B:_____

1

A:_____

B:_____

A:_____

B:_____

III.   LEARNING THE DIALOG

After the presentation of the dialog (see pages xviii–xix) help your teacher memorize it. Do not let up until he or she has it word-perfect.

IV.   ROLE-PLAYING

How would you say the dialog in the situations below?

A. B is very shy and A is very outgoing.

B. A and B are obviously very interested in each other.

C. B is very aloof and disinterested until she hears that A's mother's surname is the same as hers.

V.   VOCABULARY

Familiarize yourself with the following words needed to change the dialog. Ask your teacher to help you pronounce them correctly. Remember that accented vowels are long.

A. Divisions of the day.

bigat	morning (approximately daybreak until late morning)
aldaw	midday (approximately eleven to one o'clock)
malem	afternoon (approximately early afternoon until dusk)
rabii	evening, night (approximately dusk until daybreak)

B. Terms of respect.

Áding	Younger sister or brother
Mánang	Older sister

2

Mánong	Older brother
Nána	Aunt
Táta	Uncle
Balásangko	My young lady
Barok	My young man
Nakkong	My child
Nánang	Mother
Tátang	Father
Lélang	Grandmother
Lélong	Grandfather
Ápong	Grandparent
Ápo	Sir or Madam

C. Pronouns (See Glossary for the full set.)

KO set (Genitive Pronouns)

-ko / -k	my
-mo / -m	your (singular)
-na	his, her
-yo	your (plural or polite singular)

VI. CHANGING THE DIALOG

A. Using the situations below, and referring to the vocabulary section that you have just studied, how would you change:

PART 1 of the dialog?

1. B is A's {
male neighbor, five years older than himself.
uncle.
aunt.
grandmother.
boss.
sixty-year-old laundry woman.
mother.
father.
child.
niece.
nephew.
}

3

2. It is
$\begin{cases} \text{8:00 a.m.} \\ \text{9:00 p.m.} \\ \text{12:30 p.m.} \\ \text{5:00 p.m. (and getting dark).} \\ \text{11:00 a.m.} \\ \text{3:00 p.m.} \end{cases}$

Part 2 of the dialog?

1. B's first name is
$\begin{cases} \text{Lucia.} \\ \text{Mariano.} \\ \text{Caridad.} \\ \text{Lorenzo.} \\ \text{Rosie.} \end{cases}$

2. B's last name is
$\begin{cases} \text{Torio.} \\ \text{Gomez.} \\ \text{de la Cruz.} \\ \text{Bragado.} \end{cases}$

3. B's full name is
$\begin{cases} \text{Rosita Rafael.} \\ \text{Lourdes Enrico.} \\ \text{Loreto Asuncion.} \\ \text{Rudy Tolentino.} \\ \text{Esperanza Marcos.} \end{cases}$

B. How would you change the dialog in the situations below?

1. It is 7:00 at night. Both A and B are male strangers.

2. It is 11:30 in the morning. A is older than B.

3. It is 3:00 in the afternoon. A is younger than B. They are females.

4. B gives her full name the first time she is asked for it.

5. The surname of A's father is Santiago.

VII. QUESTION AND ANSWER

Get a partner and practice asking and answering these questions with him or her. Try asking other questions, too. Ask your teacher to give you the Ilokano for words you do not know. Speak only in Ilokano.

1. Ania ti nágan ni B?

4

2. Ania ti apelyído ni B?

3. Ania met ti apelyído ni Nánang ni A?

VIII.   NOTES

    A.   Grammar

        1.

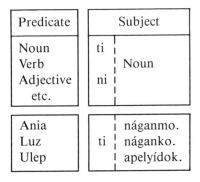

Predicate	Subject	
Noun Verb Adjective etc.	ti ni	Noun

Predicate		Subject
Ania Luz Ulep	ti	náganmo. náganko. apelyídok.

In English, a subject occurs before a predicate.

Subject	Predicate
My surname	is Sagucio.

In Ilokano, a predicate occurs before a subject.

Predicate	Subject
Sagucio	ti apelyídok.

    In English verbs are the most common predicates. In Ilokano, many kinds of words and phrases, such as nouns, verbs, adjectives, and question words can be predicates.

    In English, when we want to describe a noun which is the subject of a sentence, we must use a linking verb like is or are:

    In Ilokano, there are no linking verbs. The noun (or adjective) which is used to describe the subject is itself the predicate.

    Subjects which are common nouns like *nágan* and *apelyído* are usually introduced by *ti:*

        Maria ti náganko.

5

When *ti* is used in this way, it is a subject determiner.

If the subject were a personal noun like *Luz* or *Juan,* it would be introduced by *ni:*

Amerikáno ni David.

Other subject determiners also occur. You will learn them later.

2.

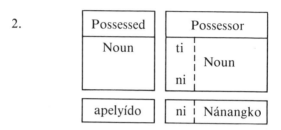

In English, a possessor can precede the thing that is possessed, John's dog (John is possessor, dog is possessed.), or it may follow, The dog of John. In Ilokano, a possessor can only follow a possessed noun, *áso ni Juan.* Possessors, like subjects, are introduced by either *ti* or *ni. Ti* is used if the possessor is a common noun, *áso ti Amerikáno, ni* is used if it is a personal noun, *aso ni Juan.* Words like *Nánangko* (my mother) which name kinship relationships, are personal nouns in Ilokano, as though they were people's names. The determiners which introduce a possessor noun phrase are called genitive determiners.

3.

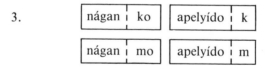

A possessor can be a pronoun instead of a noun phrase. In Ilokano, these pronouns, called genitive or KO set pronouns, are attached to the end of the Possessed noun.

The pronouns meaning my and your have two forms. When the Possessed noun ends in a consonant, *-ko* and *-mo* are used. When it ends in a vowel, *-k* and *-m* are used.

B. Culture

Terms Of Respect

1. Ilokanos are very careful to show respect when speaking to someone, especially if that person is older or is of a higher

social status than the speaker. An Ilokano would never say simply, *Naimbag a bigatmo* (Good morning) without adding the hearer's title, *Mis,* or a relationship term, *Áding* (Younger brother or sister) or *Mánang* (Older sister). All of the terms of respect listed in the Vocabulary section, except *Nánang* (Mother) and *Tátang* (Father), are commonly used with people who are not your real relatives, but are about the same age as the relatives with whom you would normally use the term. So a teenager about fifteen years old would address a twenty-year-old young man as *Mánong* (Older brother) and a woman who is about his mother's age as *Nána* (Aunt). He would address a twelve-year-old boy or girl as *Áding.*

2. Ilokanos also show respect by using the plural pronoun *-yo* (your [plural]) when addressing older people, strangers, and people of higher social status than themselves. A student for example, should always greet his teacher Good morning by saying, *"Naimbag a bigat**yo**, Maestra."* It is less acceptable to say, *"Naimbag a bigat**mo**, Maestra."*

IX. EXERCISES

A. Complete the sentences by putting time words and terms of respect in the blank spaces.

   1. a: Naimbag a _____ mo, _____.

     b: Naimbag a _____ yo met, _____.

   2. a: Naimbag nga _____ yo, _____.

     b: Naimbag nga _____ mo met, _____.

   3. a: Naimbag a _____ m, _____.

     b: Naimbag a _____ yo met, _____.

   4. a: Naimbag a _____ yo, _____.

     b: Naimbag a _____ mo met, _____.

B. Underline the subject once and the predicate twice.

   1. Elsie ti náganko.

   2. Ania ti apelyídom?

   3. Taga-Manilaak.

4. Elvira ti nágan ni Mánangko.

5. Amerikáno ni David.

C. Fill in the blanks with the correct determiners.

1. Ania _____ nágan _____ Nánangmo?

2. Espinelli _____ apelyídok.

3. Pilipíno _____ Lélongko.

4. Bragado _____ apelyído _____ áding _____ Juanita.

5. Rafael _____ apelyído _____ Táta Lucas.

D. Attach the pronouns to the nouns which precede them. Make any changes in the pronouns that are necessary.

1. malem mo _____   2. apelyído ko _____

    nágan ko _____   rabii mo _____

    aldaw mo _____   ápo ko _____

    bigat mo _____   trabáho mo _____

    Nánang mo _____

    Lélang ko _____

E. Answer the following questions in Ilokano.

1. Ania ti nágan ni Tátangmo?

_____.

2. Ania ti apelyído ni Nánangmo?

_____.

3. Alma Gomez ti náganko. Ania met ti náganmo?

_____.

X.   COMMUNICATION ACTIVITY

Greet your classmates in Ilokano. Then, introduce to the class the classmates whose names you remember. Ask your teacher for any words in Ilokano needed to make the introductions.

Lesson Two

I. DIALOG: Making Friends

Study the following dialog. Try to understand the meaning of each sentence by referring to the literal translations of the words on the right.

1

1.	A:	Taga-anóka?	taga-anóka	from-where-you
2.	B:	Taga-Kalihi-ak.	taga-Kalihi-ak	from-Kalihi-I
			sadinno	where
3.	A:	Sadinno idiay Kalihi?	idiay	there (far)
			paggigianam	place-staying-you
4.	B:	Idiay Kalihi-Uka.	ita	now
			met	also
		2	agtrabtrabáhoka	working-you
			wen	yes
5.	A:	Paggígianam ita?	ngem	but
6.	B:	Idiay met Kalihi.	partaym	part-time
			láeng	only
7.	A:	Agtrabtrabáhoka?	ala	alright
8.	B:	Wen, ngem partaym láeng.	kastá	like-that
			pay	moreover
		3	papanam	place-go-you
			mapának	go-I
9.	A:	Papanam ita?	agtrabáho	to work
			ngarod	then
10.	B:	Mapának agtrabáho	la	all right
11.	A:	Kastá pay ngarod.		
12.	B:	Ala wen la.		

II. TRANSLATING THE DIALOG

Write a free translation of the dialog (i.e., a translation in natural English). Do it in pencil, and then check it against the translation in Appendix One. Make whatever corrections are necessary.

A:_____

B:_____

9

A:_____

B:_____

A:_____

B:_____

A:_____

B:_____

A:_____

B:_____

A:_____

B:_____

III.   LEARNING THE DIALOG

After the presentation of the dialog, get a partner and help each other memorize it. You have five minutes to do this.

IV.   ROLE-PLAYING

How would you say the dialog in the situations below?

A. A and B meet on the bus. A is in front and B is in back.

B. A and B are in the theater. The movie is going on. B gets ready to go.

C. A is persistent and B is obviously in a hurry.

D. A and B meet at a party. The place is very noisy. They introduce themselves to each other before beginning the dialog.

E. A is a policeman and B is a motorcyclist. B is being apprehended by A.

V.   VOCABULARY

Familiarize yourself next with the following words that you will need to use in the next sections. Ask your teacher to help you pronounce them correctly. Remember that accented vowels are longer than other vowels.

A. Nouns

1. places

balay	house, home
baybay	beach, ocean, sea
eskuéla	school
kapiteria	cafeteria
kláse	class
laybrari	library
opisina	office
simbáan	church
síne	movie theater, movie
tiendáan	store

2. objects

adóbo	pork or chicken dish with spices and vinegar
asaymen	assignment
bolpen	ballpoint pen
danom	water
diario	newspaper
hálu-hálo	confection of mixed shaved ice and sweets
inumen	drink
kanen	food
lápis	pencil
libro	book
relo	watch
papel	paper
pisarra	blackboard
sapátos	shoes
sinílas	slippers

B. Verbs

1. AG-

agádal	to study
agbása	to read, to go to school
agdígos	to go swimming, to take a bath
aginana	to take a rest
agpasiar	to go for a stroll, to go out
agsála	to dance
agsiáping	to go shopping
agsúrat	to write
agwatwat	to exercise

2. -UM-

dumáwat	to ask for (something)
gumátang	to buy
uminom	to drink

3. MANG-

mangála	to get
mangan	to eat

4. MA-

matúrog	to sleep

5. PANG--AN

pangaláan	place for getting
panganan	eating place

6. Negatives

saan	no, not
awan	none

C. Pronouns (See Glossary for the full set.)

AK set (subject pronouns)

-ak	I
-ka	you (singular)

| ø, isu, isúna | he or she |
| -kayo | you (plural or polite singular) |

The absence of a pronoun is interpreted as meaning he or she.

D. Locative Demonstratives

ditoy	here
dita	there (near)
idiay	there (far)

E. Idioms/Expressions

| Ala wen la. | Okay. |
| Diak ammo. | I don't know. |

F. Vocabulary Horse Racing Sweepstakes

Rules:
1. The class divides into teams of four horses.

2. Each horse is assigned a number from one to four.

3. The horses arrange themselves in rows, so that horse #1 is in the first row, horse #2 is in the second row (see diagram).

4. The rows race in sequence, that is row 1 precedes row 2, and does not race again until row 4 has raced.

5. A race takes place when the race master (the teacher) selects a card at random from a prepared set of vocabulary index cards and presents the English word to the racing row.

6. A horse wins a race by being the first to give the correct Ilokano equivalent for the English word.

7. Only one response can be given for each race. If it is correct, the team scores and a new vocabulary item is presented for the next race.

8. If an incorrect answer is given, the next race is run immediately using the same vocabulary item.

9. Scoring depends upon the number of races needed to produce a correct answer. If a correct answer is given on the

first race, one point is added to the team score, if on the second race, two points are added, and so on.

10. Incorrect answers penalize the team. An incorrect answer on a first race deducts one point from the team score, if on the second race, two points are deducted, and so on.

11. The winning team is the one that scores the highest number of points.

	Team I	Team II	Team III	Team IV	Team V	Team VI
Horse #1 (Umuna a Kabalio)						
Horse #2 (Maikadua a Kabalio)						
Horse #3 (Maikatlo a Kabalio)						
Horse #4 (Maikapat a Kabalio)						

VI.   CHANGING THE DIALOG

A. Using the situations below, and referring to the vocabulary section that you have just studied, how would you change:

PART 1 of the dialog?

1. B is from
- Vigan, Ilocos Sur.
- Mako St. in Mililani.
- 7th Avenue in Kaimuki.
- Minneapolis, Minnesota.
- Stockton, California.
- Seattle, Washington.
- Agana, Guam.
- Cotabato, Philippines.
- Pangasinan.
- Ilagan, Isabela.

14

PART 2 of the dialog?

1. B lives in
$\begin{cases} \text{Salt Lake, on Likini St.} \\ \text{Aiea, on Kaamilo St.} \\ \text{1055 Gulick St., Apt. \#2.} \\ \text{Hawaii Kai, on Lunalilo Home Road.} \\ \text{Ewa Beach.} \end{cases}$

PART 3 of the dialog?

1. B is going
$\begin{cases} \text{swimming.} \\ \text{shopping.} \\ \text{to eat.} \\ \text{to take a rest.} \\ \text{to have a sleep.} \\ \text{to dance.} \\ \text{to take a walk.} \\ \text{to exercise.} \\ \text{to take a bath.} \\ \text{to study.} \end{cases}$

2. B is going
$\begin{cases} \text{to buy shoes.} \\ \text{to eat some adobo.} \\ \text{to buy a newspaper.} \\ \text{to read a book.} \\ \text{to have a drink of water.} \\ \text{to write his assignment.} \\ \text{to eat halu-halo.} \\ \text{to get something to drink.} \\ \text{to get some food.} \end{cases}$

A:	Papanam?
B:	Mapának gumátang ti sapátos.

3. B is going
$\begin{cases} \text{to church.} \\ \text{to the store.} \\ \text{to the beach.} \\ \text{to school.} \\ \text{to class.} \end{cases}$

4. B is going
$\begin{cases} \text{swimming at the beach.} \\ \text{shopping at Ala Moana.} \\ \text{to eat at King Tsin.} \\ \text{to rest at home.} \\ \text{to nap in the library.} \end{cases}$

B. How would you change the dialog in the situations below?

1. A does not live in Kalihi, nor is he from Kalihi.

2. A is from Kauai and lives in Waipahu.

3. A is an old man, a neighbor of B, who is a high school girl.

4. B is a female neighbor of A, thirty-five years older than himself.

5. B does not have a job.

6. D and C are talking about A and B, instead of the latter conversing.

7. In Parts 1 and 2, A is asking about B's mother.

VII. QUESTION AND ANSWER

Get a partner and practice asking and answering these questions with him or her. In addition, try asking other questions. Ask your teacher to give you the Ilokano for words you do not know. Speak only in Ilokano.

1. Taga-ano ni B?

2. Taga-ano ni B idiay Kalihi?

3. Paggígianan ni B?

4. Agtrabtrabáho kadi ni B?

5. Papanan ni B?

VIII. NOTES

A. Grammar

1.

Predicate	Subject
Noun Verb Adjective Other parts of speech	-AK pronoun
taga-ano taga-Kalihi agtrabtrabáho mapan	-ka -ak -ka -ak

16

A single word in Ilokano can express a whole sentence. When the subject of a sentence is a pronoun it is joined on to the end of the predicate, e.g., *Maestró-ak* (I am a teacher) and *Estudianteka* (You are a student). (The third person singular pronoun *isu* or *isúna* are separate words, however.) The pronouns which are used to express the subject are the *-AK* set. The complete set of *-AK* pronouns is given in the glossary at the back of the text.

2.

	prefix	root
noun	taga-	Kalihi
verb	ag-	trabáho
adjective	na-	imbag

In English we frequently build words using prefixes and suffixes, un- is a prefix on unknown, and unsure; -ing is a suffix on seeing and knowing. Ilokano uses many prefixes and suffixes when building its nouns, verbs and adjectives.

a. *taga-*(person from) is a prefix which can be attached to any place name. It forms another noun.

b. *ag-* is one of the many prefixes that form verbs. It can be attached to roots that are verb-like, such as *takder* (stand) to form *agtakder* (to stand up), *Agtakderka!* (Stand up!). It can also be attached to many noun-like roots, such as *sapátos* (shoes), to form *agsapátos* (to wear shoes), *Agsapátoska!* (Put shoes on!).

Other verb-forming prefixes are *mang-* and *ma-*.

The differences between these prefixes is subtle and for the time being it is better to learn which prefix most commonly occurs with which roots.

Some verbs commonly use *-um-* rather than *ag-, mang-,* or *ma-,* such as *gumátang* (to buy), and *uminom* (to drink). Notice that *-um-* is inserted into a word that begins with a consonant. It always immediately precedes the first vowel. For example:

g-um-átang	to buy
b-um-úlod	to borrow
d-um-áwat	to ask for
um-inom	to drink
um-ísem	to smile
um-útang	to owe

c. *na-* is a prefix that forms adjectives. It is attached to a large number of roots such as *imbag* (good), *sayáat* (fine), to form adjectives: *naimbag, nasayáat.*

3.

Location	
ditoy	Locative
dita	noun
idiay	

A location phrase tells us where an action takes place, or where the object or person being described is. The main word in this kind of phrase is the locative noun, like Hawaii or *eskueláan* (school). When it is introduced by the location word *ditoy*, it places the location near the speaker, *ditoy Hawaii* (here in Hawaii). If it is introduced by *dita,* it places the location away from the speaker but in the near vicinity, *dita eskuelaan* (there in the school [near us]). If it is introduced by *idiay,* it places the location in the distance, *idiay Pilipinas* (there in the Philippines [away from us]).

4. Questions. There are two main kinds of questions in Ilokano, just as in English.

a. One kind is called a Yes-No question. The appropriate answer to such a question is either yes or no:

	English	Ilokano
Question:	Do you work?	Agtrabtrabáhoka?
Answer:	Yes.	Wen.
Question:	Are you from here?	Taga-ditoyka?
Answer:	No.	Saan.

In English, a Yes-No question is different from its equivalent statement in several ways, including the addition of verbs like do, and the position of the subject (after do, not before it). In Ilokano, a Yes-No question is just the same as

18

its equivalent statement, except for its intonation. Compare the intonation lines on the following sentences, and have your teacher read them so you can hear the difference.

Statement: Agtrabtrabáhoka. You are working.

Question: Agtrabtrabahoka? Are you working?

b. The other kind of question is called an Information Question, because it seeks information, usually by using such words as What, Who, Where, When, and Why. In English this kind of question is sometimes called a Wh-Question. In Ilokano, information questions have the question word in the predicate. The subject contains the thing being inquired about:

	Predicate	Subject	
what	ania	ti	common noun
who	sinno	ti	common noun
where	sadinno	ti	place noun

Examples:

1. Ania ti trabáhona?   What is his work?

2. Sinno ti maestráyo?   Who is your teacher?

3. Sadinno ti papanam? Where are you going?

Sentences like 3 above are usually shortened by eliminating the first two words, so that a location question usually consists simply of a location word:

Papanam?   Literally: Place-of-your-going?

Paggígianam?   Literally: Place-of-your-living?

Question words such as these are commonly used, so in the following section, we will examine the way they are constructed.

5. Locative Gerunds. A gerund is a word which started life as a verb, but has been changed into a noun:

papanan   place of going, destination

paggígianan   place of living, residence

Both of these words are based on verb roots, *pan* (go) and *gian* (stay), but after they have been prefixed and suffixed, they have become nouns. Because there are complexities in the analysis and description of these two common words, simpler forms will be used to illustrate the formation of locative gerunds.

pag-	Verb	-an
pag-	trabahu	-an
pag-	adál	-an
pag-	digús	-an
pag-	gian	-an

Verbs which can be formed with *ag-*, become locative gerunds when *pag-* is prefixed, and *-an* is suffixed to the root. Thus, *agádal* (to study), becomes *pagadálan* (place for studying), and agdígos becomes *pagdigusan* (place for taking a bath).

pang-	Verb	-an
pang-	alá	-an
pang-	(k)an	-an

Similarly, verbs which can be formed with *mang-* become locative gerunds when *pang-* is prefixed, and *-an* is suffixed to the root. Thus, *mangan* (to eat) becomes *panganan* (place for eating) and *mangála* (to get) becomes *pangaláan* (place for getting).

(The k of *kan* is not pronounced when prefixed with either *mang-* or *pang-*, i.e., *mang-* + *kan* becomes *mangan* and *pang-* + *kan* becomes *pangan*.)

Any word which ends in an *-an* suffix, changes *-an* to *-ak* (i.e., *-an* + *ko*) for my and *-an* to *-am* (i.e., *-an* + *mo*) for your:

my working-place   pagtrabahuak   (pagtrabahuan + ko)

your working-place   pagtrabahuam   (pagtrabahuan + mo)

Locative gerunds always take the genitive or *KO*-set of pronouns when they are possessed as in the above examples, just as in English we use possessive pronouns such as my or your. They do not take the -*AK* or subject set because the pronoun is not the subject of the sentence.

IX. EXERCISES

A. 1. Attach *ag-* to the following words.

takder	_____	to stand up
taray	_____	to run
kanta	_____	to sing
lúgan	_____	to ride
sao	_____	to speak
ádal	_____	to study

2. Insert -*um*- into the following words.

gátang	_____	to buy
búlod	_____	to borrow
sápol	_____	to look for
sungbat	_____	to answer
inom	_____	to drink
útang	_____	to owe
ísem	_____	to smile
ay	_____	to come

3. Attach prefix *pag-* and suffix -*an* to the following words.

síne	_____	movie theater
kláse	_____	classroom
trabáho	_____	working place
gian	_____	residence, place to stay
eskuéla	_____	school

gátang   _____   place for buying

ruar   _____   exit, outside

B. Combine the gerund and the pronoun into one word, changing the form of the suffix and the pronoun as necessary.

paggianan + ko   _____

pageskueláan + ko   _____

pagturúgan + ko   _____

pagwatwátan + ko   _____

pagdawátan + mo   _____

panganan + mo   _____

pangaláan + mo   _____

papanan + mo   _____

C. Answer 1, 3, and 4 in the positive and 2 and 5 in the negative.

1. Taga-La Unionka?   _____

2. Aginanákayo?   _____

3. Gumátang ti sapátos?   _____

4. Mapankayo mangan idiay restawran?   _____

5. Ditoy ti pagsaláam?   _____

D. Fill in the blanks in the following sentences with the appropriate word or phrase.

1. Idiay Waipahu ti _paggígianak_. I live in Waipahu.

2. Ditoy Honolulu ti _____. I work here in Honolulu.

3. Dita kapiteria ti _____. I eat at the cafeteria.

4. Idiay balayna ti _____. I am going to his house.

5. Ditoy sála ti _____. I sleep in the parlor.

6. Dita baybay ti _pagpasiáram_. You take a walk on the the beach.

22

7. Dita lamisáan ti _____. You write on the table.

8. Dita sofa ti _____. You sit on the sofa.

9. Idiay Ala Moana ti _____. You go shopping at Ala Moana.

10. Idiay gardenmi ti _____. You get some flowers from our garden.

E. Add a subject pronoun to the following words to make a complete sentence. (Refer to Appendix I.1 for the full *AK* set.) Remember to join all but the third person singular pronoun (he, she) to the predicate.

1. Ilokano _____.
   I
   I am Ilokano.

2. Maestro _____.
   he
   He is a teacher.

3. Taga-Luzon _____.
   she
   She is from Luzon.

4. Agtrabáho _____.
   we (excl.)
   We will work.

5. Gumátang _____ ti sábong.
   we (incl.)
   Let us buy some flowers.

6. Estudiante _____ ditoy Hawaii?
   you (sing.)
   Are you a student here in Hawaii?

7. Saan _____ nga agam-ammo?
   you (pl.)
   Don't you know each other?

8. Agilokáno _____.
   we (dual)
   Let's speak Ilokano.

9. Aginggles _____.
   they
   They speak English.

10. Agtaksi _____.
    we (excl.)
    We will take a taxi.

F. Translate the following sentences.

1. Abogádo-ak. _____

2. Taga-Kailua ak. _____

3. Mapankayo idiay opisína. _____

4. Agtrabtrabáho-ak idiay _____
   kapiteria.

5. Mapának mangan ti saymin. _____

6. Agádalka ti leksionmo. _____

7. Estudiantéka ditoy? _____

8. Mapankami agsiáping. _____

9. Gumátangtayo ti libro. _____

10. Mapanta agpasiar. _____

11. Mapan matúrog. _____

12. Mapanda gumátang ti relo. _____

13. Taga-ano ni Ádingmo? _____

14. Bumúlodka ti papel. _____

15. Umísemkayo. _____

G. Rearrange the following scrambled sentences.

1. -ak/idiay/maestro/   Maestró-ak idiay Waipahu.
   Waipahu.   I am a teacher in Waipahu.

2. Ewa Beach/Lino/   _____
   taga-/ni.   Lino is from Ewa Beach.

3. Hilton/agtrabtrabáho/ _____
   idiay/-ka?   Do you work at the Hilton?

4. -mo/taga-/Nánang/   _____
   ni/-ano.   Where is your mother from?

5. isúna/balay/mapan/   _____
   idiay/-yo   He/She will go to your house.

6. Kailua/sadinno/   _____
   pagtrabtrabahuam/   Where in Kailua do you work?
   ti/idiay?

24

7. agpasiar/-ak/mapan/
   baybay/dita.   _____
              I am going to take a walk
              on the beach.

8. gumátang/mapan/
   Lisa/ni/libro/ti.   _____
              Lisa will go and buy a book.

9. agad-ádal/-ka/
   Kalakaua/idiay?   _____
              Are you studying on Kala-
              kaua?

10. estudiante/mapan/ti/
    matúrog.   _____
              The student will go to sleep.

11. idiay/-ak/Pilipinas/
    ageskuéla.   _____
              I go to school in the Philip-
              pines.

12. eskuéla/libro/ti/ti/
    pangaláan/idiay/-da. The school is where they will
              get a (some) book(s).

13. danom/-kayo/ti/
    uminom.   _____
              (You-plural) drink some water.

14. ti/mangan/-tayo/
    hálu-hálo.   _____
              Let's eat some halo-halo.

15. -ka/lápis/mangála/ti. _____
              (You-singular) get a pencil.

H. Answer the following questions in Ilokano. Write your answers
   in the right column.

   1. Taga-anóka?   _____

   2. Agbasbásaka?   _____

   3. Pagbasbasáam?   _____

   4. Agtrabtrabáhoka? _____

   5. Pagtrabtrabahuam? _____

   6. Ania ti trabáhom? _____

7. Paggígianam? _____

8. Pangpanganam? _____

X.   COMMUNICATION ACTIVITY

A. Get to know your classmates and write the name of:

1. someone who has the same first initial as yourself. _____

2. someone who is from the same place as you are. _____

3. someone who lives in the same area as you do. _____

4. someone who works. _____

5. three people who are from the same area as you.
_____
_____
_____

6. two people who are from outside the State.
_____
_____

7. someone who has the same job as you. _____

Tell the class about the people you have just met.

B. Divide into pairs and take turns talking about the people in the chart on the following page. Ask your partner questions, such as:

Sadinno ti pagbasbasáan ni Manuel Diaz?	Where does Manuel Diaz go to school?
Ania ti trabáhona?	What is his work?
Sinno ti awan trabáhona?	Who does not have a job?
Sinno ti saan nga agbasbása?	Who does not go to school?

26

Nágan	Pages-eskueláan / Pagbasbasáan	Pagtátaengan/ Paggígianan	Trabáho	Pagtrabtrabahuan
Manuel Diaz	Aiea High School	Kaamilo St., Aiea	diánitor	Luke and Duke's Ice Cream
Lucio Paz	Unibersidad ti Hawaii	Manoa	maestro	Kalakaua Intermediate School
Irma de Leon	Farrington High School		kahéra	Barrio Fiesta Supermarket
Julieta Ramos	Leilehua High School	Waipahu	weytres	Gánas Restaurant
Elsa Opinaldo	McKinley High School	Kapahulu		
Marcos Santos Mario	Leeward Community College	Pearlridge	weyter	Pulon's Restaurant
Domingo	Kapiolani Community College	Palama	kusinéro	Pansiteria Líwliwa
Elvira Bagain	Unibersidad ti Hawaii	Hawaii Kai		
Luz Asuncion		1011 Nuuanu Ave.	secretaria	City Hall
Alma Macugay		1213 School St.	doktóra	Luna Hospital

XI.   WRITING PRACTICE

A. Write about a person you have just met, giving as much personal information as you can using what you have learned from the last two lessons. Start by telling his name. Remember to use third-person pronouns, ø, **isuna** or **isu** and **-na** where appropriate.

B. Read about a prominent Filipino woman or heroine and introduce her to the class, giving as much information about her as you can.

C. Read about a prominent Filipino man or hero and introduce him to the class, giving as much information about him as you can.

Lesson Three

I. DIALOG: Introducing a Friend

Study the following dialog. Try to understand the meaning of each sentence by referring to the literal translations in the box.

1

1. A: Agam-ammókayo?
2. B: Saan, saankami nga agam-ammo.

2

3. A: Lino, ni Lisa daytoy. Kasinsinko. Lisa, ni Lino daytoy. Kaeskueláak iti "History."
4. B: Kumustáka, Lisa?
5. C: Naimbag láeng. Ket sika?
6. B: Naimbag met.

3

7. C: Taga-ditoyka?
8. B: Saan, taga-Maui-ak.
9. C: Ay, taga-Maui-ak met!
10. B: Aya? Sadinno idiay Maui?

agam-ammókayo	be-acquainted with-each-other-you (plural)
saan	no
saankami	not-we (exclusive)
agam-ammo	be-acquainted with-each-other
daytoy	this
kasinsinko	cousin-my
kaeskueláak	fellow-student-my
kumustáka	how-you (singular)
naimbag	fine
láeng	just
ket	and
sika	you
taga-ditoyka	from-here-you
taga-Maui-ak	from-Maui-I
ay	oh
met	also
aya	is that so
sadinno	where

II. TRANSLATING THE DIALOG

Write a free translation of the dialog (i.e., a translation in natural English). Do it in pencil, and then check it against the translation in Appendix One. Make whatever corrections are necessary.

A:_____

B:_____

A:_____

_____

B:_____

C:_____

B:_____

C:_____

B:_____

C:_____

B:_____

III.   LEARNING THE DIALOG

After the presentation of the dialog, divide into groups of three. One of you will listen carefully while the other two read the dialog to each other. Take turns in reading and listening until each of you has memorized all the parts.

IV.   ROLE-PLAYING

How would you say the dialog in the situations below?

A. B and C used to go steady. This is the first time they have seen each other since they broke up. They are both nervous. A does not know about their past.

B. B is apparently attracted to C, and A is trying to be possessive. C is acting flirtatious.

C. A, B, and C are at a party. The party is very noisy.

V. VOCABULARY

Familiarize yourself with the following words that you will need to use in the following sections. Ask your teacher to help you pronounce them correctly.

A. Nouns

1. Occupations

abogádo	lawyer
artista	filmstar
bos	boss
dentista	dentist
doktor	doctor
inhiniéro	engineer
maestro/a	teacher
nars	nurse
sekretaria	secretary

2. Relationships

a. Kinship

abalayan	parent of one's child's spouse
anak	child
asáwa	spouse
baket	wife, old woman
íkit	aunt
ípag	sister-in-law
kaanakan	niece or nephew
kabsat	sibling (brother or sister)
kapidua	second cousin
kasinsin	cousin
katugángan	parent-in-law
káyong	brother-in-law
lakay	husband, old man
manúgang	son/daughter-in-law

dadakkel	parents	
uliteg	uncle	

b. Other relationships

gayyem	friend
kaarrúba	neighbor
kabbalay	housemate
kaeskueláan	classmate
katrabahuan	co-worker

c. Reciprocal relationships

agabalayan	*abalayan* of each other
agassáwa	husband and wife
agípag	sisters-in-law
aggayyem	friends of one another
agkaarrúba	neighbors of one another
agkabagian	relatives
agkabbalay	housemates
agkabsat	brothers, sisters of one another
agkaeskueláan	classmates of one another
agkaopisináan	officemates
agkasinsin	cousins of one another
agkatrabahuan	co-workers
agkatugaw	seatmates

B. Adjectives

madi	bad, not good
nasayáat	fine, well

C. Pronouns (See Appendix I.1 for the full set.)

AK set (subject pronouns)

-da	they

D. Demonstratives

daytoy	this
dayta	that (near)
daydiay	that (far away)

32

E. Idioms

kastoy latta   not so well; so-so; literally, 'like this only'

VI.   CHANGING THE DIALOG

A. Using the situations below, and referring to the vocabulary section that you have just studied, how would you change:

PART 1 of the dialog?

1. A asks B if B and C are
$\begin{cases} \text{relatives.} \\ \text{siblings.} \\ \text{husband and wife.} \\ \text{neighbors.} \\ \text{second cousins.} \\ \text{co-workers.} \\ \text{classmates.} \\ \text{sisters-in-law.} \\ \text{cousins.} \\ \text{friends.} \\ \text{housemates.} \\ \text{officemates.} \\ \text{seatmates.} \end{cases}$

PART 2 of the dialog?

1. A's friend's name is
$\begin{cases} \text{Carlina.} \\ \text{Mila.} \\ \text{Angel.} \\ \text{Rusty.} \\ \text{Luke.} \\ \text{Jesus.} \end{cases}$

2. His classmate's name is
$\begin{cases} \text{Carlos.} \\ \text{William.} \\ \text{Enchong.} \\ \text{Erlinda.} \\ \text{Jose.} \\ \text{Arsenia.} \end{cases}$

3. Lisa is A's $\left\{\begin{array}{l}\text{friend.} \\ \text{cousin.} \\ \text{second cousin.} \\ \text{secretary.} \\ \text{teacher.} \\ \text{boss.}\end{array}\right.$

4. Lino is A's $\left\{\begin{array}{l}\text{classmate in Ilokano.} \\ \text{co-worker at Pacific Insurance.} \\ \text{neighbor.}\end{array}\right.$

5. Lisa is $\left\{\begin{array}{l}\text{not feeling the best.} \\ \text{feeling fine.} \\ \text{feeling terrible.}\end{array}\right.$

PART 3 of the dialog?

1. B is from $\left\{\begin{array}{l}\text{Kauai.} \\ \text{Kona.} \\ \text{Abra.} \\ \text{Isabela.} \\ \text{Tarlac.} \\ \text{Alaska.} \\ \text{Los Angeles.} \\ \text{Waialua.} \\ \text{Lanai.} \\ \text{Molokai.} \\ \text{Stockton.} \\ \text{Cotabato.}\end{array}\right.$

B. How would you change the dialog in the situations below?

1. Lisa is A's younger sister; Lino is a classmate of A in mathematics; Lisa is not from Maui.

2. Lisa is A's teacher.

3. Lino and Lisa have met before.

4. Lisa is A's mother who is also his teacher.

VII.   QUESTION AND ANSWER

Get a partner and practice asking and answering these questions with him or her. In addition, try asking other questions. Ask your teacher to give you the Ilokano for words you do not know. Speak only in Ilokano.

1. Agam-ammo kadi da A ken C?
2. Sinno ni Lisa?
3. Sinno ni Lino?
4. Sinno ni A?
5. Taga-ano da Lisa ken Lino?
6. Kaarúba ni A ni Lisa?
7. Kaeskueláan ni Lino ni A?
8. Agkabsat da A ken Lino?
9. Agkapin-ano da A ken Lisa?
10. Ket da Lino ken Lisa, agkapin-anóda?

VIII. NOTES

A. Grammar

1.

Predicate	Subject
Reciprocal Verb	Plural Noun or Pronoun

Agam-ammó Agkabsat	-kayo -da

In English, when we use a reciprocal verb such as to be acquainted with or to know, we must use the words one another or each other. In Ilokano, it is sufficient to use a plural noun or a plural pronoun as the subject. The verb itself, with prefix -ag expresses reciprocity:

Agam-ammo   -da. They know each other.
da Lisa ken Lino. Lisa and Lino know each other.
dagiti estudiante. The students know each other.

35

Relationship terms like *kabsat* also become reciprocal when *ag-* is attached to them:

	-kayo. You (plural) are siblings.
Agkabsat	da Ben. Ben (and his companion[s]) are siblings.
	dagiti kaduána. Her/His companions are siblings.

2. Plural Determiners. *ti* and *ni* are generally used for nouns which are singular. Their corresponding plural forms are *dagiti* and *da,* as in the chart:

	sg	pl
common	ti	dagiti
personal	ni	da

when *da* is used before a personal noun, *da Ben,* it refers to two or more people one of whom is called Ben. So it can be translated as Ben and his friend[s], or Ben and his companion[s]. The names of any additional people can also be mentioned, *Da Ben, Lisa, ken Maria* (Ben, Lisa, and Maria).

The use of plural determiners with common nouns is only necessary when the plurality needs to be made explicit. In some sentences, even though the noun is plural, only *ti* may be used:

Gimmátangda ti áso.	{ They bought a dog, or
	They bought some dogs.

However, if the plural noun is the subject of a sentence, the plural marker *dagiti* will usually be used:

Agpasiar dagiti kabbalayko.	My housemates will go for a walk.
Ginátangda dagiti áso.	They bought the dogs.

3. *Ka-* noun *-an* means one associated with the noun.

ka-eskuelá-an	fellow student, classmate
ka-kuartu-an	roommate
ka-opisiná-an	officemate

36

| ka-trabahu-an | fellow worker |
| ka-bagi-an | relative ('fellow body') |

4. Non-kin relationship terms such as those in 3 above (*kaeskueláan,* etc.) also become reciprocal when *ag-* is attached to them.

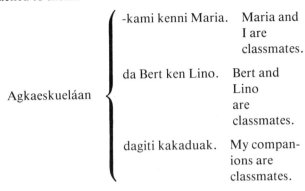

Agkaeskueláan	-kami kenni Maria.	Maria and I are classmates.
	da Bert ken Lino.	Bert and Lino are classmates.
	dagiti kakaduak.	My companions are classmates.

5. Negatives.

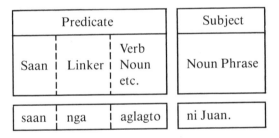

Predicate			Subject
Saan	Linker	Verb Noun etc.	Noun Phrase
saan	nga	aglagto	ni Juan.

A positive sentence like *Agam-ammo da Lisa ken Lino* can be made into a negative sentence by placing the negative word *saan* at the beginning of the sentence. It is always linked to the verb with one of the linkers *a* or *nga:*

Positive: Agam-ammo da Lisa ken Lino.
Lisa and Lino know each other.

Negative: Saan nga agam-ammo da Lisa ken Lino.
Lisa and Lino do not know each other.

Positive: Aglagto ti ubing.
The child will jump.

Negative: Saan nga aglagto ti ubing.
The child will not jump.

Positive: Agkabsat da Juan ken Jose.
Juan and Jose are brothers.

Negative: Saan nga agkabsat da Juan ken Jose.
Juan and Jose are not brothers.

A noun which occurs in the predicate can also be made negative in the same way:

Positive: Amerikano ni Juan.
John is an American.

Negative: Saan nga Amerikano ni Juan.
John is not an American.

Any pronoun which occurs with the word which is the predicate is moved so that it attaches to *saan*. There are two situations when this can occur. The first is the moving of a genitive (*KO* set) pronoun from a predicate noun on to *saan:*

Positive: Gayyemko ni Marta.
Marta is my friend.

Negative: Saanko a gayyem ni Marta.
Marta is not my friend.

The second is when a subject (*AK* set) pronoun attached to a predicate verb is moved on to *saan*. In a case like this the subject pronoun occurs in the middle of the predicate:

Positive: Agtrabáho-ak.
I'll work.

Negative: Saának nga agtrabáho.
I won't work.

6. Linker.

Negative	Lk	Verb
Saan	nga	agam-ammo.

Adjective	Lk	Noun
Naimbag	nga	adlawmo.

38

There are several places in Ilokano grammar where words must be joined by a linker. Two of these places (after *saan,* with adjectives) have already been introduced, and are illustrated above. Others will appear later in the text.

There are two forms of the linker, *nga* and *a*. *Nga* is used if the next word begins with a vowel, *a* is used if the next word begins with a consonant, e.g.,

Saan nga aglagto ni Juan.
Juan will not jump.

Saan a naglagto ni Juan.
Juan did not jump.

Naimbag nga aldawmo.
Good day.

Naimbag a rabiim.
Good evening.

B. Culture

Ilokanos seem to be more aware of second and third cousins (*kapidua* and *kapitlo*) than are English speakers. For most English speakers, their second cousins are the children of their first cousins, which makes them a generation younger than themselves. In Ilokano, your second cousins are the children of your parents' first cousins. They are therefore in your generation, not your children's generation. Similarly, your third cousins are the grandchildren of your grandparents' first cousins and are also at your generation level. Your second and third cousins are addressed in Ilokano as though they were your own siblings, with the appropriate terms of respect, *Mánong* (older brother), *Mánang* (older sister) or *Áding* (younger brother or sister). Similarly, the first cousin of one of your parents would be called *Táta* or *Nána* (Uncle or Aunt), and the first cousin of one of your grandparents would be called *Lélong* or *Lélang,* or simply *Ápong.*

IX. EXERCISES

A. Underline the subject once and the predicate twice in the following sentences. Remember that a third person singular subject (i.e., he or she) may not appear.

1. Saának nga agsapátos ita.

   I will not wear shoes today.

2. Saan nga agádal (isúna).

   She/He will not study.

3. Saan nga aggayyem da Flora ken Fe.

   Flora and Fe are not friends.

4. Saanko nga am-ammo ni Lorenzo.

   I do not know Lorenzo.

5. Saankami a mangan.

   We will not eat.

6. Saan nga agláko ni Naty ita.

   Naty will not sell today.

7. Saan nga agpasiar.

   She/He will not go for a walk.

8. Saan a Pilipino dagiti estudiante.

   The students are not Filipinos.

9. Saan nga agípag da Yoly ken Rita.

   Yoly and Rita are not sisters-in-law.

10. Saanko a kapidua ni Elping.

    Elping is not my second cousin.

11. Saankami nga agkapidua.

    We are not second cousins.

12. Saanda nga agkasinsin.

    They are not cousins.

13. Saanda a kasinsin ni Emer.

    Emer is not their cousin.

14. Saanmi a kapitlo ni Ramon.

    Ramon is not our third cousin.

15. Saankami nga agkapitlo.

    We are not third cousins.

B. The following sentences need a linker to make them grammatical. Rewrite the sentences with the linker in its correct position.

1. Saan Amerikano ni Julita. _____

2. Saanda agabalayan. _____

3. Saan agádal (isúna). _____

4. Saankami mangan. _____

5. Saának mapan agtrabáho. _____

C. Write the correct form of the determiner in the following sentences. Choose from *ni, da, ti* and *dagiti*.

1. Agkabsat _____ Ben ken Vit.

2. Mapan matúrog _____ balásang.

3. Taga-ditoy _____ Apo Mayor.

4. Agsála _____ Regina (and her companions).

5. Agkasinsin _____ kaarrúbak.

6. Saan nga agam-ammo _____ estudiante.

D. Answer the following questions in Ilokano.

Kapin-ano ni Juan ti . . .   What is the relation of
                                   these people to Juan?

1. anak ti kabsatna?   child of his brother or
                                   sister?

   Kaanakanna. _____

2. Tátang ti kasinsinna?   father of his cousin?
   Ulitegna. _____

3. Nánang ti kasinsinna?   mother of his cousin?

   _____

4. anak ti ulitegna?   child of his uncle?

   _____

5. anak ti kasinsinna?   child of his cousin?

   _____

6. asáwa ti kabsatna a laláki?   wife of his brother?

   _____

7. asáwa ti kabsatna a babái?   husband of his sister?

   _____

8. asáwa ti anakna?   spouse of his child?

   _____

9. dadakkel ti asáwana?   parents of his spouse?

   _____

10. dadakkel ti asáwa ti anakna?   parents of his child's
                                          spouse?

    _____

11. anak dagiti dadakkelna?   child of his parents?

    _____

12. Nánang ti anakna?   mother of his child?

    _____

E. Give the reciprocal verb forms of the following nouns.

   1. kabagian   agkabagian   to be relatives
      relative

   2. kaeskueláan   _____   to be classmates
      classmate

   3. katrabahuan   _____   to be fellow workers
      fellow-
      worker

   4. kaopisináan   _____   to be officemates
      office-mate

   5. kagrupuan   _____   to be group-mates
      group-mate

   6. kaarrúba   agkaarrúba   to be neighbors
      neighbor

42

7. kabbalay   _____   to be housemates
   housemates

8. katugaw   _____   to be seatmates
   seat-mate

X.   COMMUNICATION ACTIVITY

A. Walk around the classroom. Take a friend and introduce him or her to another friend.

B. You are the ambassador of the Philippines to the United States. You and a Philippine Consul are attending a function. You introduce him to another ambassador or consul.

C. Find someone who is from the same place as you. Continue the conversation and get more personal information about him.

D. 1. Divide into groups of three.
   2. Write a continuation of the dialog in seven minutes.
   3. Practice the dialog including what you have written for five minutes.
   4. Say the dialog with a partner without using your notes. The third member of your group will act as your prompter.

E. 1. Read the puzzle.

   Mánong ni Nila ni Dante.
   Mánang ni Dante ni Nora.
   Áding ni Nora ni Miguel.
   Áding ni Miguel ni Bito.
   Áding ni Bito ni Dante.

   2. a. Sinno ti inauna a laláki?   Who is the oldest brother?

   b. Sinno ti inauna a babái?   Who is the oldest sister?

   c. Sinno ti in-inauna, ni Miguel wenno ni Dante?   Who is older, Miguel or Dante?

   d. Sinno ti in-inauna, ni Nora wenno ni Nila?   Who is older, Nora or Nila?

e. Manóda nga agkakabsat? How many brothers and sisters are they?

3. Write the names of the siblings in order, from the oldest to the youngest. Number them.

XI. WRITING PRACTICE

A. Write a short narrative explaining the relationships in the dialog among A, Lisa and Lino.

B. Each student will think of a sentence containing *ag-* and *pag—an* or *pang—an* verbs and write it on the board until a coherent dialog is created.

XII. LISTENING PRACTICE

Listen carefully as the teacher reads the following story to you. She will ask you questions about the story.

Taga-Ilokos ni Luna. Taga-Ilokos met ti gayyemna. Pablo ti nágan ti gayyemna. Agkeaeskueláanda idiay McKinley High School.

Idiay Waialua ti paggígianan ni Pablo. Idiay met ti paggígianan ni Luna. Agkaarrúbada idiay Waialua.

Saan nga agkatrabahuan da Luna ken Pablo. Agtrabtrabáho, ni Pablo idiay "Dole Pineapple Company". Saan nga agtrabtrabáho ni Luna.

Naiyanak da Pablo ken Luna idiay Vigan. Idiay met ti nakaiyanakan dagiti dadakkelda.

Agam-ammo dagiti dadakkel da Pablo ken Luna.

New words:

naiyanak   was born

nakaiyanakan   place where someone was born

44

Lesson Four

I. DIALOG: Discovering Ethnic Origins

Study the following dialog. Try to understand the meaning of each sentence by referring to the literal translations in the box.

1

1. A: Insikka?

2. B: Saan, Amerikáno, Kastíla, ken Pilipíno-ak.

2

3. A: Sinno ti Kastíla iti pamiliáyo?

4. B: Ni Nánangko. Kastíla ti apelyídona.

5. A: Ania ti apelyídona?

6. B: Enriquez.

7. A: Ay, mestísoka, gáyam!

8. B: Wen, mestíso-ak.

3

9. A: Sinno met ti Amerikáno iti pamiliáyo?

10. B: Siak. Naiyanákak ditoy.

11. A: Ay, kasta?

Insikka	Chinese-you
saan	no
Amerikáno	American
Kastíla	Spanish
ken	and
Pilipíno-ak	Filipino-I
sinno	who
pamiliáyo	family-your (plural)
Nánangko	mother-my
apelyídona	surname-her
ania	what
ay	oh
mestísoka	mestizo-you
met	also
siak	I
naiyanákak	born-I
ditoy	here
gáyam	so (discovery)
kasta	like-that

II. TRANSLATING THE DIALOG

Write a free translation of the dialog (i.e., a translation in natural English). Do it in pencil, and then check it against the translation in Appendix One. Make whatever corrections are necessary.

A:_____

B:_____

A:_____

B:_____

A:_____

B:_____

A:_____

B:_____

A:_____

B:_____

A:_____

III.   LEARNING THE DIALOG

After the presentation of the dialog, close your books and build the dialog line by line, each student taking a turn. If you cannot remember your line, your classmates may prompt you. Afterwards, two students will say the dialog to each other.

IV.   ROLE-PLAYING

How would you say the dialog in the situations below?

A. A is speaking boisterously, and B is embarrassed but tries to be polite.

B. A and B are at the cafeteria at the airport. A plane has just landed and is creating a tremendous roar.

C. A is very friendly, but B is acting pretentious and affected.

V.   VOCABULARY

Familiarize yourself with the following words that you will need to use in the following sections. Ask your teacher to help you pronounce them correctly.

A. Nationalities

Amerikáno/a	American
Hawayáno/a	Hawaiian
Italiáno/a	Italian
Meksikáno/a	Mexican
Aleman	German
Bietnamis	Vietnamese
Hapon	Japanese
Indian	Indian
Indonísian	Indonesian
Inggles	English
Insik	Chinese
Kastíla	Spanish
Maykronísian	Micronesian
Portuges	Portuguese
Pranses	French
Samuan	Samoan

B. Pronouns

AK set (subject pronouns)

-kami	we (exclusive)

SIAK set (predicate set)

siak	I
dakami	we (exclusive)
dakayo	you (singular, polite or plural)

VI.   CHANGING THE DIALOG

A. Using the situations below, and referring to the vocabulary section that you have just studied, how would you change:

PART 1 of the dialog?

1. B is
$$\left\{\begin{array}{l}\text{Filipino.}\\\text{Chinese.}\\\text{American.}\\\text{Mexican.}\\\text{Hawaiian.}\\\text{Portuguese.}\\\text{German.}\end{array}\right.$$

2. B is
$$\left\{\begin{array}{l}\text{American-Chinese.}\\\text{Filipino-English.}\\\text{Filipino-Italian.}\\\text{German-American.}\\\text{French-Vietnamese.}\\\text{Indian-Chinese.}\\\text{Samoan-Filipino.}\\\text{Hawaiian-Filipino.}\end{array}\right.$$

3. A is speaking to B with deference.

4. A is in B's house and is talking to his brothers and sisters.

PART 2 of the dialog?

1. B's mother is
$$\left\{\begin{array}{l}\text{German.}\\\text{Chinese.}\\\text{Japanese.}\\\text{Mexican.}\\\text{American.}\end{array}\right.$$

2. B's father is
$$\left\{\begin{array}{l}\text{Indian.}\\\text{Samoan.}\\\text{Hawaiian.}\\\text{Vietnamese.}\\\text{Italian.}\\\text{French.}\end{array}\right.$$

3. B's grandfather was
$$\left\{\begin{array}{l}\text{Spanish.}\\\text{English.}\\\text{Chinese.}\end{array}\right.$$

4. B's grandmother was
$$\left\{\begin{array}{l}\text{Portuguese.}\\\text{Hawaiian.}\\\text{Filipino.}\end{array}\right.$$

PART 3 of the dialog?

1. B was born in
{
Hawaii.
Samoa.
Japan.
the Philippines.
Germany.
Micronesia.
Mexico.
China.
Spain.
Indonesia.
France.
}

B. How would you change the dialog in the situations below?

   1. B has a different ethnic makeup from what is stated in the dialog.

   2. B is A's new boss who is considerably older than he is.

VII.   QUESTION AND ANSWER

Get a partner and practice asking and answering these questions with him or her. In addition, try asking other questions. Ask your teacher to give you the Ilokano for words you do not know. Speak only in Ilokano.

   1. Insik ni B?

   2. Ania ni B?

   3. Amerikáno ti apelyído ti nánang ni B?

   4. Amerikáno ti apelyído ti tátang ni B?

   5. Sinno ti mestíso?

   6. Sinno ti Amerikáno?

   7. Sinno ti Pilipíno?

   8. Ápay nga Amerikáno ni B?

VIII.   NOTES

A. Grammar

1.

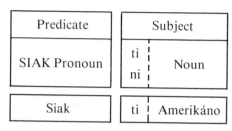

When a pronoun is used as the predicate of a sentence, the predicate or *SIAK* pronoun set is used. The complete set of *SIAK* pronouns is given in the Glossary.

Notice the difference in meaning between the following two sentences.

a.   Siak ti Amerikáno.   I am the American.

b.   Amerikáno-ak.   I am American.

The first sentence answers the question *Sinno ti Amerikáno?* (Who is the American?). The response, *Siak* (I), must occur as the predicate.

The second sentence answers the question *Aniáka?* (What are you?). The response, *Amerikáno,* must occur as the predicate.

2. Ilokano has three pronouns that are not distinguished in English. These will be explained here using the *SIAK* set, but the *AK* set and the *KO* set also contain pronouns with the same meanings.

a.   English uses you whether you are speaking to one person or to more than one. In Ilokano *sika* (you) is restricted to one person; *dakayo* (you) is normally used for plural, but can be used for singular if the speaker is being polite.

       sika   you (singular)

       dakayo   you (plural), or you (singular, polite)

b.   In English, the pronoun we can be used if the speaker is talking about himself and his friends and not including the person he is speaking to. Or it may include the hearer. In Ilokano, three different pronouns are used to mean we.

> *data* we two. This pronoun is used if the speaker <u>includes</u> only one other person with him.

> *datayo* we all. This pronoun is used if the speaker <u>includes</u> the person, or persons who are listening to him.

> *dakami* we not you. This pronoun is used if the speaker <u>excludes</u> the person or persons who are listening to him.

3. Negative Questions And Their Responses. A negative question is formed just like a negative statement, using *saan,* but with different intonation:

> a. Saanka nga Amerikáno.
> You are not an American.

> b. Saanka nga Amerikáno?
> Are you not an American?

The response to a negative question is somewhat tricky to an English speaker. In English, if you were to answer a question like b. above with "No," it would mean you were not an American. In Ilokano, if you were not an American you would answer either *Wen, saának nga Amerikáno* (Yes, I am not an American) or *Saan, saának nga Amerikáno* (No, I am not an American). On the other hand, if you disagree with the question because you are an American, you would answer either *Wen, Amerikáno-ak* (Yes, I am an American) or *Saan man, Amerikáno-ak* (Not so, I am an American).

Negative Question

> a. Agreeing Response: Wen, or Saan

> b. Disagreeing Response: Wen, or Saan man

The two words *saan man* are usually pronounced as one word *samman.*

4. Many Ilokano words which have been borrowed from Spanish, such as *Amerikáno* and *maestro,* have two forms, one which ends in *o,* which is used to refer to males *(abogádo),* and one which ends in *a,* which is used to refer to females *(abogáda).*

5. Sentence Modifiers. There are a number of little words which occur in Ilokano which are somewhat like adverbs. These little words are often hard to define, and have several meanings. Two have been introduced so far:

   a. *met* also, too. This word indicates a kind of shift, such as a switch in speakers, or referents:

   Ket sika met, ngay?
   And what about you?

   Sinno met ti Amerikáno iti pamiliáyo?
   And who's the American in your family?

   It can also mean contrary to an assertion,

   Adda dita lamisáan ti sapátosmo.
   Your shoes are on the table.

   Awan met ditoy.
   But they're not here.

   or expectation,

   Kunak no Kastílaka ket saan met gáyam.
   I thought you were Spanish, but you're not.

   b. *gáyam* so. This word is often used when the speaker suddenly becomes aware of something or when he is reminded of something. In English we might say, Oh, yes now I remember! or Now I see!

B. Culture

   1. Probably the majority of Filipinos have Spanish surnames. This is not necessarily because they had a Spanish ancestor. When the Spanish began their rule in the Philippines over four hundred years ago, most Filipinos had only one name, which is still the custom in some of the smaller ethnic groups in the mountains of the Philippines as well as in parts of Indonesia. So the Spanish gave out surnames which have remained with many Filipinos until today.

2. The term 'mestizo' is a Spanish term meaning someone of mixed racial ancestry. In the Philippines the term particularly refers to someone who is part Spanish and part Filipino. It has a good connotation and is not derogatory. A mestizo generally has lighter skin than other Filipinos, a quality which is much admired.

IX.   EXERCISES

A. Rearrange the words to make grammatical sentences.

1. Samuan/isúna/ti

_____
He is the Samoan.

2. siak/Pilipíno/ti

_____
I am the Filipino.

3. -ak/Pilípino

_____
I am Filipino.

4. Mr. Hidalgo/dakayo/ ni

_____
Are you (singular, polite) Mr. Hidalgo?

5. ti/estudiante/sika

_____
You (singular) are the student.

6. -ka/estudiante

_____
You are a student.

7. ti/dakayo/maestra

_____
You (singular, polite) are the teacher.

8. -kayo/maestra

_____
You (polite) are a teacher.

9. maestra/ni/ Mrs. Aquino

_____
Mrs. Aquino is a teacher.

10. maestra/ti/ni/
    Mrs. Aquino   _____
                               Mrs. Aquino is the teacher.

11. Melita/ni   _____
                               She is Melita.

12. Amerikáno/saan/
    nga/-ak   _____
                               I am not American.

13. Amerikáno/saan/a/
    siak/ti   _____
                               I am not the American.

14. Pilipinas/-kami/taga-   _____
                               We (exclusive) are from the
                               Philippines.

15. Pilipínas/dakami/
    taga-/ti   _____
                               We (exclusive) are the ones
                               from the Philippines.

B. Underline the correct pronoun in each of the sentences. ø
   means does not appear.

   1. (Ak, Siak) ti Ilokáno.

   2. Amerikáno ken Pilípino (siak, -ak)

   3. Saan (dakayo, -kayo) nga Aleman?

   4. (Isúna, ø) ti Hapon, (siak, -ak) ti Pilipíno.

   5. (Sika, -Ka) ti Pranses, (-da, isuda) ti Insik.

   6. (Data, -Ta) ti mestíso.

   7. Kastíla ti apelyídomi, ngem Pilipíno (dakami, -kami).

C. Write an answer to the following questions selecting from the
   list of names those that would be appropriate to the nationality.

            McArthur   Nguyen
            Nagata   de Gaulle
            Ching   Marcos
            Luafa   del Prado
            Carvalho

1. Sinno ti Rúso?   Who is the Russian?

   Ni Kruschev ti Rúso.   Kruschev is the Russian.

2. Sinno ti Kastíla?

_____

3. Sinno ti Portuges?

_____

4. Sinno ti Pranses?

_____

5. Sinno ti Pilipíno?

_____

6. Sinno ti Bietnamis?

_____

7. Sinno ti Amerikáno?

_____

8. Sinno ti Samuan?

_____

9. Sinno ti Hapon?

_____

10. Sinno ti Insik?

_____

D. Answer the question below indicating the nationality of the persons whose names appear on the left column.

Ania dagitoy a tattáo?   what are these people?

1. ni McArthur   _____

2. ni Nagata   _____

3. ni Ching   _____

4. ni Luafa   _____

5. ni Carvalho   _____

6. ni Nguyen   _____

7. ni de Gaulle   _____

8. ni Marcos   _____

9. ni del Prado   _____

10. ni Sharma   _____

X.   COMMUNICATION ACTIVITY

A. Take a map of the world and describe where the different ethnic groups are found.

B. Take a map of the world and describe where each of your ancestors were born, where they lived, or where they came from.

C. Take a map of the Philippines and describe where each of your ancestors were born, where they lived, or where they came from.

D. Take a map of Hawaii and indicate where different ethnic groups are located.

XI.   WRITING PRACTICE

A. In a letter to your friend, you gave him ten pieces of information about yourself and some members of your family. List them below.

1. _____

2. _____

3. _____

4. _____

5. _____

6. _____

56

7._____

8._____

9._____

10._____

XII. LISTENING PRACTICE

A. Listen for markers in the sentences. Identify them and the nouns with which they go.

1. Ania ti náganmo?

2. Cruz ti apelyído ni káyongko.

3. Taga-ano ni Lisa?

4. Dita Alapai ti pagbasbasketbólanmi.

5. Mapan agtrabáho da Helen ken Carmen.

6. Agtes dagiti estudiante.

7. Saan nga agam-ammo da Mister Santos ken Mis Libed.

8. Nasingpet ni Apo Mayor.

9. Laláki ti kaarrúbak.

10. Agpaspasiar dagiti aggayyem.

11. Idiay Kalihi ti paggígiananmi.

12. Agkabagian da James Sales ken Abner Sales.

13. Agad-ádal daydiay lakay.

14. Mapának idiay balayyo.

15. Agbasbásaak ditoy Unibersidad ti Hawaii.

16. Dita kapiteria ti pangpanganak.

17. Sika ti gayyemko.

18. Ni Mr. Gomez ti maestrok.

19. Matúrog da Lolita ta nabannogda.

20. Daytoy laláki ti abogádo.

Lesson Five

I.

DIALOG: Telling Time, Likes and Dislikes

Study the following dialog. Try to understand the meaning of each sentence by referring to the literal translations in the box.

1

1. A: Sinno ti maestrom iti Matemátiks?

2. B: Ni Mr. Lucas.

3. A: Ay, kayatko ni Mr. Lucas. Nalaing ken nasingpet pay.

4. B: Úray siak met. Kayatko met ni Mr. Lucas.

5. A: Ápay?

6. B: Wen, ta istrikto únay ngem nakakatkatáwa.

2

7. A: Ay, ania ti órasen?

8. B: Alas dos y médian.

9. A: Ay, óras ti klásekon!

3

10. B: Ápay, ania nga óras ti klásem?

11. A: Alas dos y média. Innakon ta naládawakon.

12. B: Inka ngarúden.

13. A: Ala, kastá pay ngarod.

14. B: Kastá pay.

sinno	who
maestrom	teacher-you
kayatko	like-I
nalaing	clever, bright, good, sharp
nasingpet	kind, nice
pay	moreover
úray	even
siak	I
met	also
ápay	why
ta	because
istrikto	strict
únay	very
ngem	but
nakakatkatáwa	funny
ania	what
órasen	time-already
alas	hour
dos	two
y	and (Spanish)
médian	half-already
óras	time
klásekon	class-my already
klásem	class-your
innakon	go-I-already
naládawakon	late-I-already
inka	go-you
ngarúden	then-already
ala	okay
kasta	like-that

II. TRANSLATING THE DIALOG

Write a free translation of the dialog (i.e., a translation in natural English). Do it in pencil, and then check it against the translation in Appendix One. Make whatever corrections are necessary.

A:_____

B:_____

A:_____

B:_____

A:_____

B:_____

A:_____

B:_____

A:_____

B:_____

A:_____

B:_____

A:_____

B:_____

III. LEARNING THE DIALOG

After the presentation of the dialog, divide into groups of two. Teach your partner the dialog. When he has learned it, let him teach you. Do this for five minutes. Afterward, select a partner from another group and say the dialog with him or her.

IV. ROLE-PLAYING

How would you say the dialog in the situations below?

A. A and B are chatting in front of the school. They are both blowing bubble gum.

B. A and B are talking loudly in front of a classroom. The teacher comes out several times to stop them.

C. The bell has rung and A is in a hurry to go to class, but B keeps talking even after A has started to walk away.

V. VOCABULARY

Familiarize yourself with the following words that you will need to use in the following sections. Ask your teacher to help you pronounce them correctly.

A. Nouns

eksámen	exam
míting	meeting
padaya	party
pangaldaw	lunch
paria	bittermelon
trabáho	work

B. Adjectives

ababa	short
kalbo	bald
naalas	ugly
naános	kind, patient
nagaget	diligent, industrious
naguápo	handsome
naimbag	good, fine
nakuttong	skinny
nalaing	smart, good, clever
nanumo	humble
napait	bitter
napintas	pretty, beautiful

60

napúdaw	fair-skinned
naragsak	happy
nasadot	lazy
nasayáat	nice, good
nasingpet	nice, kind
nasírib	intelligent
natangsit	proud
nataráki	handsome
natáyag	tall
naunget	cranky
naurnos	organized, tidy
bastos	gross, rude
istrikto	strict
kábaw	absentminded
nakabutbuteng	scary
nakakatkatáwa	funny
tarabítab	talkative

C. Adverbs

únay	very

D. Conjunctions

ken	and
ngem	but
ta	because

VI. CHANGING THE DIALOG

A. Using the situations below, and referring to the vocabulary section that you have just studied, how would you change:

PART 1 of the dialog?

1. Mr. Lucas is A's teacher in { Ilokano. Literature. Tagalog. History. English.

2. Mr. Lucas is
- handsome and smart.
- patient and organized.
- smart and funny.
- tall and fair-skinned.
- handsome and industrious.

3. Mr. Lucas is
- strict but smart.
- strict but funny.
- handsome but lazy.
- smart but cranky.
- short but handsome.
- bald but handsome.

4. A and B don't like Mr. Lucas

because he is
- cranky.
- strict.
- lazy.
- talkative.
- gross.

> A: Ay, diak kayat ni Mr. Lucas! Naunget únay ken istrikto.
>
> B: Úray siak met. Diak met kayat ni Mr. Lucas.

because he is
- smart but too strict.
- hardworking but too cranky.
- handsome but too short.
- nice but very lazy.

5. A and B don't like Mr. Lucas

because he is
- not diligent.
- not patient.
- not organized.
- not sharp.
- not nice.

PART 2 of the dialog?

1. The time is already
- 2 P.M.
- 12 noon
- 1 P.M.
- 11:15 A.M.
- 5:15 P.M.
- 9:30 A.M.
- 1:30 P.M.
- 3:45 P.M.
- 6:45 P.M.
- 8:45 P.M.

2. A's class starts at
$\begin{cases} \text{1:05 P.M.} \\ \text{4:10 P.M.} \\ \text{3:20 P.M.} \\ \text{6:25 P.M.} \\ \text{2:35 P.M.} \\ \text{5:40 P.M.} \\ \text{8:50 A.M.} \\ \text{7:55 A.M.} \end{cases}$

PARTS 2 and 3 of the dialog?

1. It is time
   for A's
   $\begin{cases} \text{work.} \\ \text{exam.} \\ \text{lunch.} \\ \text{meeting.} \end{cases}$

2. It is time for
   A and his com-
   panion's (use
   -mi instead
   of **-ko**)
   $\begin{cases} \text{work.} \\ \text{exam.} \\ \text{lunch.} \\ \text{meeting.} \\ \text{party.} \end{cases}$

B. How would you change the dialog in the situations below?

1. The setting is at work rather than at school.

2. A's class is in the morning.

3. Neither A nor B likes Mr. Lucas.

4. A is asking about B's teacher in another subject.
   It is midday. A is going to a meeting.

5. B is an old man, a classmate of A's.

6. B's responses, where appropriate, are negative.

VII. QUESTION AND ANSWER

Get a partner and practice asking and answering these questions with him or her. Try asking other questions, too. Ask your teacher to give you the Ilokano for words you do not know. Speak only in Ilokano.

1. Sinno ti maestro ni B iti Matematiks?
2. Sinno ni Mr. Lucas?
3. Sinno ti mayat kenni Mr. Lucas?
4. Ápay a kayat da A ken B ni Mr. Lucas?
5. Ania nga óras ti kláse ni A?
6. Papanan ni A?
7. Ápay nga agap-apura ni A?

VIII.   NOTES

A. Grammar

1.

Location	
iti	Common Noun

iti	pamilíayo
iti	matemátiks

Real locations, like places, are usually introduced by *ditoy, dita,* and *idiay.* Locations which are more abstract such as family and mathematics are usually introduced by *iti.* This determiner has many uses in Ilokano, all of which can be broadly characterized as locative, or having to do with location.

2.

Interrogative Predicate		Subject	
a. Interrogative Word or b. Interrogative Phrase (Int. Lk. Noun)		ti	Sentence (-Subject)

a.	Ania	ti	kayatko
b.	Ania a síne	ti	kayatko

64

Interrogatives such as *ania* (what) and *sinno* (who) can be modified to request specific information. In English, for example, we say Which movie? or What house? In Ilokano, an interrogative is modified by joining the modifier (e.g., person, or house) to the interrogative word with a linker, either *a* or *nga*. A sequence of interrogative-linker-noun forms an interrogative phrase:

a. Ania a kuarto ti pagklasiantayo?
What room will we have our class in?

b. Sinno nga estudiante ti umay?
Which student will come?

If the expected response of an interrogative sentence is a personal noun (such as *ni Juan*), the question word is always *sinno* rather than *ania,* regardless of whether it is best translated as who, what or which.

3. Telling Time. Spanish numerals are used in Ilokano for telling time. A list which can be used for this purpose is included in the Glossary.

The word *alas* (from Spanish a las "on the") is used before all of the hours except one o'clock, when *ala* is used:

ala úna	one o'clock
alas dos	two o'clock
alas tres	three o'clock
etc.	

The Spanish *y* (and), pronounced *i,* is used before quarter and half hour expressions:

alas tres y kuárto	three o'clock and a quarter (3:15)
alas tres y média	three o'clock and a half (3:30)

However, it is generally absent if minutes are expressed in numbers:

alas tres síngko	3:05
alas tres kínse	3:15
alas tres bainte-dos	3:22
alas tres kuarénte-síngko	3:45

After the half hour, time may be expressed as in the last example, or the following expression may be used:

ménos kínse para alas kuátro
four o'clock less fifteen minutes (3:45)

4. *-EN* already, now. This little sentence modifier is very common. It has two forms, *-en* occurs after a consonant, and *-n* occurs after a vowel. When *-n* attaches to a pronoun which would otherwise lose its final vowel, the vowel is retained, e.g.,

kláse-k
klase-ko-n

kláse-m
kláse-mo-n

5.

Predicate	Agent	Subject
Patient Focus Verb	*KO* set Pronoun *ti/ni* Noun	*AK* set Pronoun *ti/ni* Noun

All verbs which have *ag-, mang-,* and *-um-* (and a few verbs which have *ma-*) attached to them can be called actor focus verbs. In other words, the actor of the action is the subject of the sentence. However, when a verb has a patient (sometimes called an object) which is a pronoun, a personal noun or a definite noun phrase (that is, one which can be translated with the, but not a), Ilokano always makes the patient the subject of the sentence, e.g.,

Predicate	Agent	Subject	
Kayat-ko		ni Juan.	I like John. (John is liked by me.)
Kayat-ko		isúna.	I like him.
Kayat-ko		ti libro.	I like the book.

Verbs, like *kayat,* which indicate that the subject of the sentence is not the Actor but is the patient, are called

66

patient-focus verbs. Notice the word order, predicate first, agent second, subject (patient) third. Notice also that the agent pronouns are the same set that is used for possessor. This is why the *KO* set is sometimes called genitive, because it is used for agents as well as possessors.

IX.   EXERCISES

A. Add a locative word or determiner to the following sentences.

1. Saanka a mapan _____ balay?
                            over there

2. Gumátangtayo ti gasolína _____Shell.
                                          here

3. Sinno ti Ilokano _____ pamiliáyo?
                            in

4. Sinno ti kaeskueláam _____Music.
                                  in

5. Agmeriendáak _____ alas tres.
                        at

6. Matúrogkayo _____ alas dies.
                        at

7. Umútangtayo _____ tiendáan.
                     there (near)

8. Mapankami _____ padaya.
                      to

9. Sinno ti mapan _____míting?
                          to

10. Ageksámentayo _____ Ilokano.
                            in

B. Translate the following sentences into Ilokano.

1. What time is it?   _____

2. Which lesson is that?   _____

3. What time is your class?   _____

4. Which doctor is your
   cousin?
   _____

5. What time is our snack
   break?
   _____

C. Write the times in Ilokano.

12:00 (noon)   _____

1:10 P.M.   _____

2:15 P.M.   _____

            or_____

3:25 P.M.   _____

3:45 P.M.   _____

            or_____

4:45 P.M.   _____

            or_____

5:30 P.M.   _____

D. Answer the following question in Ilokano using the cues on the
   right.

   Question: Ania ti órasen?

   Answer: _____   12:00 (noon)

             _____   2:00 P.M.

             _____   1:00 P.M.

             _____   7:30 A.M.

             _____   9:45 A.M.

_____ 10:45 A.M.

_____ 11:55 A.M.

E. 1. List five things that you like and say why you like them.

a. Kayatko ti balot ta naímas.

b. _____

c. _____

d. _____

e. _____

f. _____

2. List five people that you like and say why you like them. With some, add a term of respect before the person's name.

a. Kayatko ni Lorenzo ta naános.

b. _____

c. _____

d. _____

e. _____

f. _____

3. List five places that you like and say why you like them.

a. Kayatko ti Baguio ta napintas.

b. _____

c. _____

d. _____

69

e. _____

f. _____

4. List five things that you don't like and say why you don't like them.

    a. Diak kayat ti paria ta napait.

    b. _____

    c. _____

    d. _____

    e. _____

    f. _____

5. List five people that you don't like and say why you don't like them.

    a. Diak kayat ti káyongko ta nalóko.

    b. _____

    c. _____

    d. _____

    e. _____

    f. _____

6. List five movies that you don't like and say why you don't like them.

    a. Diak kayat ti Exorcist ta nakabutbuteng.

    b. _____

    c. _____

d. _____

e. _____

f. _____

7. List four things that you like to do and say why you like to do them.

   a. Kayatko ti matúrog ta naímas ti matúrog.

   b. _____

   c. _____

   d. _____

   e. _____

8. List four things that you don't like to do and say why you don't like to do them.

   a. Diak kayat ti mangan ti ado, ta lumukmégak.

   b. _____

   c. _____

   d. _____

   e. _____

X.   COMMUNICATION ACTIVITY

A. Study the following vocabulary in preparation for the next communication activity. Other body parts may be found in the glossary.

agong	nose
bibig	lips
buok	hair
gúrong	leg

íma	hand
kíday	eyebrow
kurimatmat	eyelash
mata	eye
múging	forehead
pingping	cheek
ngípen	teeth
rámay	fingers
takiag	arm
tengnged	neck
tímid	chin

Divide into groups of three. Consider the positive qualities of the other members of your group. Take turns in telling each one what those qualities are. For example:

Rosie, kayatka ta nagagetka, ken napintas ti matam.
Rosie, I like you because you are diligent and your eyes are pretty.

Ask your teacher to give you the Ilokano for words that you do not know. Write the qualities of each person on a piece of paper and give it to that person to keep.

B. List any negative qualities about yourself that you would like to change. Read them to your group. Your group may agree or disagree with you.

Lesson Six

I. DIALOG: Encountering an Old Friend

Study the following dialog. Try to understand the meaning of each
sentence by referring to the literal translations in the box.

1

1. A:	Ania, Pári, kumus- táka?
2. B:	Naimbag láeng, Pári. Ket sika?
3. A:	Naimbag met.
4. B:	Ala, kastá pay.

2

5. A:	Ápay nga agap- apuráka?
6. B:	Mapának agtrabáho.
7. A:	Pagtrabtrabahuam?
8. B:	Idiay "downtown". Ala, kastá pay ngarod.

3

9. A:	Kayatmo ti agmerien- da?
10. B:	Saan a mabalin, ta agtrabáho-ak. Ala, kastá pay, ket naládawakon.
11. A:	Agúrayka bassit! Anianto ti aramí- dem intuno bigat?

ania	what
Pári	friend (male)
kumustáka	how-you
naimbag	fine
láeng	just
ket	and
sika	you (singular)
met	also
ala	okay
kasta	like-that
pay	moreover
ápay	why
agap-apuráka	hurrying-you
mapának	go-I
agtrabáho	work
pagtrabtraba- huam	working place-your (singular)
kayatmo	like-you
agmerienda	have a snack
saan	not
mabalin	possible
aramídem	do-you
malem	afternoon
naládawakon	late-l-already
agúrayka	wait-you
bassit	little, small
intuno	future
bigat	morning

73

II.   TRANSLATING THE DIALOG

Write a free translation of the dialog (i.e., a translation in natural English). Do it in pencil, and then check it against the translation in Appendix One. Make whatever corrections are necessary.

A:_____

B:_____

A:_____

B:_____

A:_____

B:_____

A:_____

B:_____

A:_____

B:_____

A:_____

III.   LEARNING THE DIALOG

After the presentation of the dialog, two of you volunteer to write the dialog on the blackboard. One will write A's lines and the other, B's lines. The rest of the class will close their books and dictate the dialog to the writer. When the dialog is on the board, the teacher will read it through to you, then erase the top line. You will read the complete dialog including the missing line. The teacher will then erase the next line and the procedure will continue until the dialog is completely erased.

IV.   ROLE-PLAYING

How would you say the dialog in the situations below?

A. B is in a hurry because the bus is waiting. He has started to run but A keeps hanging on to his arm.

B. B is obviously getting impatient because he is late for work. A
is enthusiastic.

C. B is in his car. The light has turned green. A is on the sidewalk.

V.   VOCABULARY

Familiarize yourself with the following words that you will need to
use in the following sections. Ask your teacher to help you pronounce them correctly.

A. Nouns

apoynmen	appointment
bagas	uncooked rice
buksit, tian	stomach
kurtína	curtain
leksion	lesson
letra	letter
lúgan	vehicle, ride
mayor	mayor
presidente	president
prinsipal	principal
súrat	letter

B. Verbs

1. AG-

agaywan	to take care of
agbus	to take the bus
agdáit	to sew
agdiram-os	to wash face
aginom	to go drinking
aggudtaym	to have a good time
aglaba	to do laundry
aglúgan	to take a ride
agmakinilia	to type
agmerienda	to have a snack

75

agsakit	to get sick
agúray	to wait

2. -UM-

umay	to come

3. MA-

matúrog	to sleep

4. MANG- (past tense NANG-)

mamigat	to eat breakfast
mangaldaw	to eat lunch
mangrabii	to eat dinner

C. Adjectives

1. NA-

nabannog	tired
nabsog	full
nasakit	painful

2. MA-

mabisin	hungry
masakit	sick

3. No Affix

ado	many, much

VI. CHANGING THE DIALOG

A. Using the situations below, and referring to the vocabulary section that you have just studied, how would you change:

PART 1 of the dialog?

1. B is
- feeling a little off color.
- feeling bad.
- very well.

2. A is talking to
- Mr. Santos, his boss.
- a younger person.
- a very old person.
- the Mayor.
- the Principal.

76

PART 2 of the dialog?

1. B is in a hurry because

he is going
{
to read.
to study.
to sew.
to rest.
to buy rice.
to study Ilokano.
to sew his shirt.
to sew a curtain.
to read the newspaper.
to read a letter.
to sleep because he is tired.
to eat because he is hungry.
}

PART 3 of the dialog?

1. A is inviting B to
{
go swimming, but B has to go to church.
take the bus, but B is in a hurry.
wait for a ride, but B is in a hurry.
eat, but B is very full.
see a movie, but B has to study.
study at the library, but B has to babysit.
come to their house, but B has to read his lesson.
go drinking, but B's child is sick.
go swimming, but B is hungry.
go to eat, but B has a stomachache.
go for a walk, but B has a lot of work to do.
go on a vacation, but B has an exam.
eat lunch, but B has an appointment.
go out for a good time, but B has a lot of assignments.
}

B. How would you change the dialog in the situations below?

1. B is not feeling too well. He is in a hurry because he has to go to school and he is late.

2. B can't do anything that week because he has to study for an exam.

3. A is inviting B to come visit him, but B cannot because some relatives of his are coming to visit him.

4. B accepts A's invitation and pursues it.

VII.   QUESTION AND ANSWER

Get a partner and practice asking and answering the following questions with him or her. In addition, try asking other questions. Ask your teacher to give you the Ilokano for words you do not know. Speak only in Ilokano.

1. Ápay nga agap-apura ni B?

2. Sadinno ti pagtrabtrabahuan ni B?

3. Ania ti kayat ni A nga aramíden?

4. Ápay saan a mabalin a mapan agmerienda ni B?

VIII.   NOTES
A. Grammar
1. Reduplication. This word refers to a process in Ilokano which results in the repetition of part of a word. There are different kinds of reduplication and each kind has several meanings. The repetition of the first consonant (C), first vowel (V), and second consonant (C), is called CVC-reduplication:

> laglagto
> lablaba
> luglúgan

CVC-reduplication also covers words with more than one initial consonant like *trabáho,* and words which start with a vowel like *inom:*

> trabtrabáho
> in-inom
> ay-aywan
> ap-apura

When a word does not contain a middle consonant, like, *dáit* (sew) only CV- is repeated but the vowel is made long, *dádáit.*

There are two meanings for CVC- reduplication that we will consider here; these are 'continuative' and 'customary'.

a. If an action is actually going on at the time of speaking, it is a continuative action. In English, we usually translate it with is and -ing, e.g.,

agtrabtrabáho	is working
aglaglagto	is jumping
agdádáit	is sewing

b. If an action is customary and one that is usually performed, but is not necessarily being performed at the time of speaking, e.g.,

Agtrabtrabáho ni Juan.
John works. He has a job.

2.

Auxiliary	Main Verb
mapan/in- umay	Verb

There are two auxiliary verbs denoting direction in Ilokano, one meaning motion away from the speaker, *mapan* (go); the other, motion toward the speaker, *umay* (come). These auxiliaries immediately precede the main verb. No linker is used. Pronouns are always attached to the auxiliary but noun phrases follow the main verb. The auxiliary meaning go has two forms, one (which is the same as the verb to go) is *mapan*, *Mapának agtrabáho* (I'm going to work). The other is *in-*.

Although in most places *mapan* and *in-* are used interchangeably, *in-* can only be used if there is a pronoun to attach to it. *In-* cannot occur by itself in front of a verb, as *mapan* can. Either a *KO* set pronoun, or an *AK* set pronoun attaches to the auxiliary. However, when *in-* precedes a patient-focus verb, such as *aláen,* which uses the *KO* set pronoun to express the agent, a number of irregular changes occur. Compare the following sentences which have an auxiliary, with the corresponding sentences without one.

Actor-focus

a. Agdígosak.　　I'll swim.

Mapának agdígos.
Innak agdígos.　　I'll go for a swim.

b. Agdígoska.   You swim.

    Mapanka agdígos.
    Inka agdígos.   You go for a swim.

c. Agdígos.   He'll swim.

    Mapan agdígos.

Patient-focus

d. Aláek ti libro.   I'll get the book.

    Mapanko aláen ti libro.   I'll go get the
    Innak aláen ti libro.   book.

e. Aláem ti libro.   You get the book.

    Mapanmo aláen ti libro.   You go get the
    Inka aláen ti libro.   book.

f. Aláenna ti libro.   He will get the book.

    Mapanna aláen ti libro.   He'll go get the
    Inna aláen ti libro.   book.

Notice in c. above that only *mapan* may occur as the auxiliary because there is no pronoun in Ilokano which could attach to *in-*. Also notice that in d. and e. although it is the *KO* set that occurs with the verb, it is changed to the *AK* set when it is placed with *in-*. The only *KO* set pronoun that does not change when attached to *in-* is *-na*, as in f. above. Notice also that when *-ak* is attached to *in-* (as in a.), the n is doubled to give *innak*.

The auxiliary *umay* is regular, like *mapan*, e.g.,

g. Mapanmo kitáen.   Go and look at it.

h. Umaymo kitáen.   Come and look at it.

3.
Ápay	Linker	Sentence

A question which asks why is joined to the following sentence with a linker. However, in normal speech, the linker is often left out.

4. *Ken* and *ket*. These two words are commonly used conjunctions in Ilokano, both of which may be freely trans-

lated as and. Because of their similarity in meaning, they are often confused by students learning Ilokano for the first time.

Ken can join two words, two phrases or two sentences together. It is a general conjunction and implies nothing beyond the fact that what follows *ken* is simply an addition to what precedes it:

> áso ken púsa
> a dog and a cat

> dagiti nagagaget a lalláki ken napipintas a babbái
> the industrious men and the beautiful women

> Naglangoyda ken nagbaskitbolda.
> They swam and played basketball.

Notice that when joining sentences with *ken,* the first and the second parts can be reversed without any change in meaning.

With *ket,* however, what follows the conjunction is often understood as the result of what precedes the conjunction, or conversely what precedes is the purpose, or the circumstance for that which follows *ket:*

> Napanda ket nanganda.
> They left and they ate.
> (Their leaving was for the purpose of eating.)

> Awan kuartáda ket napintas ti balayda.
> They have no money and their house is beautiful.
> (Despite the circumstance of their poverty, they have a fine home.)

Ket also occurs with other meanings in Ilokano. It is the conjunction which must be used in joining numerals:

> sangagasot ket duapúlo ket dua
> one hundred and twenty two

Other uses of *ket* will be discussed as they occur in subsequent lessons.

5. Time Adverbs. There are a number of adverb-like time words which commonly occur in sentences that have continuative verbs. A number of these are joined to the verb by a linker:

81

Kanáyon a mapmapan ni Josie idiay balayda.
Josie is always going to their house.

Masansan nga agwatwatwátak.
I often exercise.

Pasaray a bumisbisíta ditoy.
She sometimes visits here.

Time words like *bigat, malem,* and *rabii* become time adverbs by inserting -*in*- before the first vowel:

binigat	every morning
minalem	every afternoon
rinabii	every night
inaldaw	every day
lin áwas	every week
binúlan	every month
tinawen	every year

These adverbs can also be joined to the verb by a linker,

Binigat nga agdigdígosak.
I take a bath every morning.

Tinawen nga agbakbakasiónak.
Every year I take a vacation.

An alternate way of expressing such time words is by using the Spanish *káda,*

káda bigat	every morning
káda tawen	every year

6.

Time	
iti intuno itay idi	Time Word

Most sentences can include a time phrase to indicate when an action takes place. General time phrases are introduced by *iti*, e.g.,

Mapan agbása ni Luz iti rabii.
Luz goes to school at night.

Phrases which specify the time in relation to the actual time when the sentence is spoken use *intuno* if future, *itay* if earlier on the same day, and *idi* if yesterday or earlier, e.g.,

    a. Mapan agbása ni Luz intuno malem.
        Luz will go to school this afternoon.

    b. Napan nagbása ni Luz itay bigat.
        Luz went to school this morning.

    c. Napan nagbása ni Luz idi rabii.
        Luz went to school last night.

Notice also that in sentences b. and c., the auxiliary and the verb begin with *n-*, which also indicates past tense.

B. Culture

The term *Pári,* freely translated "friend" or "buddy," is used as a term of address for an adult male companion, or someone to whom one wishes to extend friendship. It comes from the Spanish loanword *compadre* meaning "godfather of one's child." The female counterpart of *Pári* is *Máring* or *Mári* and originates from the Spanish loanword *comadre* meaning "godmother of one's child."

IX.   EXERCISES
   A. Answer the following questions briefly.

Ania ti ar-aramíden ni Juan idiay . . .

1. kusína?	aglutlúto	Cooking some adobo.
2. opisína?	_____	Typing a letter.
3. banio?	_____	Taking a bath.
4. kapiteria?	_____	Working.
5. laybrari?	_____	Reading a newspaper.

6. kuarto? _____ Resting.

7. gym? _____ Exercising.

8. pagsinian? _____ Watching a movie.

9. eskuéla? _____ Studying his lesson.

10. naytklab? _____ Dancing the Tango.

B. Translate the following sentences.

1. Resty always thinks.   Kanáyon nga agpan-
                               panúnot ni Resty.

2. They serenade every night. Rinabii nga agtapta-
                               patda.

3. Andres always exercises.   _____

4. Emilia sometimes waits.   (no maminsan)

                               _____

5. Esteban has a snack here   _____

   every afternoon.   _____

6. I go to the Philippines   _____

   every year.   _____

7. I wash my face every   _____

   morning.   _____

8. Teresita takes a vacation   _____

   every month.   _____

9. He gets sick every year.   _____

C. Rewrite the following sentences (where possible) using the auxiliary *in-* rather than *mapan.* Don't forget to change the pronoun where necessary. Refer to the Grammar notes.

1. Mapának aglúto.   Innak agluto.

2. Mapanda mangan.   _____

3. Mapanka man mangála ti   (stone) _____
   bato

4. Mapan agbása ni Veronica.   _____

5. Mapankami agbúya ti sine.   _____

6. Mapantayo agpiknik.   _____

7. Mapánta mangaldaw.   (to eat lunch) _____

8. Mapan ageksámen isúna.   _____

9. Mapanmo aláen ti bagmo.   _____

10. Mapanna kitáen daydiay   (to see) (ornamental _____

    masétas.   plant) _____

11. Mapanyo sapúlen ti   (look for)(ring) _____
    singsingna.

12. Mapanda lutuen ti pansit.   (noodle dish) _____

D. Translate the following sentences into Ilokano.

1. Come and see my plants.   _____

2. Come and get this dog   (áso) _____

   of yours.   _____

3. Come and eat.   _____

85

4. Will you come to work

   tomorrow?

5. Come and sleep here.

X.   COMMUNICATION ACTIVITY

A

A. You meet an old friend you haven't seen for a long time. You invite him to do something with you, but he refuses and gives reasons for his refusal. You insist and entice him. You don't take 'no' for an answer.

B

You refuse to accept your friend's invitation but he insists.

Goal for A: To get B to accept your invitation.

B   1. Divide into groups of three.

2. Write a continuation of the dialog in seven minutes.

3. Practice the dialog including what you have written for five minutes.

4. Say the dialog with a partner without using your notes. The third member of your group will act as your prompter.

Lesson Seven

I. DIALOG: Making a Date by Telephone

Study the following dialog. Try to understand the meaning of each sentence by referring to the literal translations in the box.

1

1. A: Helo.

2. B: Lisa, ni Lino daytoy.
   Daydiay gayyem ni Bert.

3. A: Sinno a gayyem ni Bert?

4. B: Daydiay kaeskueláanna
   iti "History."

5. A: Ay wen, malagipkon!

2

6. B: Anianto ti aramídem
   intuno rabii ti
   Sábado?

7. A: Awan, awan ti aramídek'.

3

8. B: Kayatmo ti agbúya ti
   síne?

9. A: Ania a síne ti buyáenta?

10. B: "Gone With the Wind."
    Intanto iti alas otso,
    mabalin?

4

11. A: Mabalin a kumúyog ni
    Ádingko?

12. B: W-w-wen. Mabalin.

daytoy	this
daydiay	that
gayyem	friend
sinno	who
kaeskueláanna	school-mate-his
wen	yes
malagipkon	remember-I-already
anianto	what-future
aramídem	do-you
intuno	future
rabii	night
Sábado	Saturday
awan	nothing
aramídek	do-I
kayatmo	like-you
agbúya	watch, view
síne	movie
buyáenta	view-we (two)
intanto	go-we (two)-future
mabalin	can
kumúyog	go-along
ádingko	younger sister/brother-my

II.   TRANSLATING THE DIALOG

Write a free translation of the dialog (i.e., a translation in natural English). Do it in pencil, and then check it against the translation in Appendix One. Make whatever corrections are necessary.

A:_____

B:_____

A:_____

B:_____

A:_____

B:_____

A:_____

B:_____

A:_____

B:_____

A:_____

III.   LEARNING THE DIALOG

After the presentation of the dialog, divide into groups of three. Two of you say the dialog to each other. If you cannot remember your line, the third member of your group may prompt you. Switch partners until each person has had a turn as prompter.

IV.   ROLE-PLAYING

How would you say the dialog in the situations below?

A. B does not want his father, who is nearby, to hear the conversation because his father is very strict.

B. B is very cautious because he is not sure how A will respond, so he sounds somewhat nervous.

C. A is very delighted to hear from B, and does not hide it.

V. VOCABULARY

Familiarize yourself with the following words which you will need to use in the following sections. Ask your teacher to help you pronounce them correctly.

A. Nouns

bisíta	visitor
nobia	girlfriend
nobio	boyfriend
padaya	party
prútas	fruits
sabsábong	flowers
sangaíli	visitor, guest

days of the week

Lúnes	Monday
Martes	Tuesday
Mierkoles	Wednesday
Huébes	Thursday
Biernes	Friday
Sábado	Saturday
Dominggo	Sunday

B. Adjectives

baro	new
dáan	old

C. Verbs

1. AG-

agála	to get, collect, gather
aglúto	to cook

89

agkol-ap	to call on the telephone
agpuros	to pick
agsagána	to prepare

D. Time words and phrases

intuno	(future time marker)
intuno bigat	tomorrow
intuno aldaw no bigat	tomorrow noon
intuno malem no bigat	tomorrow afternoon
intuno rabii no bigat	tomorrow night
intuno láwas	next week
intuno madam-dama	later on (today)
intuno malem	this afternoon
intuno rabii	tonight
ita, itatta	now, today
dágos	immediately

VI.   CHANGING THE DIALOG

A. Using the situations below, and referring to the vocabulary section that you have just studied, how would you change:

PART 1 of the dialog?

1. Lino is Bert's
{
co-worker.
neighbor.
compadre.
teacher.
older brother.
younger brother.
}

2. Lino was Bert's companion last night at the party.

PART 2 of the dialog?

1. Lino is inviting
   Lisa to go
   out on
$\left\{\begin{array}{l}\text{Saturday afternoon.}\\\text{Sunday morning.}\\\text{Monday evening.}\\\text{Tuesday noon.}\\\text{Wednesday afternoon.}\\\text{Thursday morning.}\\\text{Friday noon.}\end{array}\right.$

PART 3 of the dialog?

1. Lino wants to
   know if Lisa
   would like to
$\left\{\begin{array}{l}\text{have a snack.}\\\text{go and eat.}\\\text{go swimming.}\\\text{go get flowers.}\\\text{go pick fruits.}\\\text{buy a new car.}\end{array}\right.$

2. Lino suggests
   they
   go out
$\left\{\begin{array}{l}\text{at seven o'clock.}\\\text{right then.}\\\text{later on.}\\\text{that night.}\\\text{the next day.}\\\text{the next noon.}\\\text{the next afternoon.}\\\text{the night of the next day.}\\\text{the next week.}\end{array}\right.$

PART 4 of the dialog?

1. A asks if her
$\left\{\begin{array}{l}\text{grandmother}\\\text{older brother}\\\text{boyfriend}\\\text{guest}\\\text{friend}\\\text{co-worker}\end{array}\right\}$
can accompany them.

B. How would you change the dialog in the situations below?

1. B is Bert's co-worker. He is inviting A to see a parade on Sunday morning.

2. A has something to do on Saturday, so B suggests another day.

3. B is inviting A to go to the beach Monday afternoon.

4. A's responses are all negative where appropriate.

5. The movie is in the afternoon. A asks if her grandmother could come along.

6. B is A's math teacher.

VII. QUESTION AND ANSWER

Get a partner and practice asking and answering these questions with him or her. In addition, try asking other questions. Ask your teacher to give you the Ilokano for words you do not know. Speak only in Ilokano.

1. Sinno ti agkolkol-ap kenni Lisa?

2. Sinno ni lino?

3. Sinno ti kaeskueláan ni Lino?

4. Kaeskueláan ni Lisa ni Lino?

5. Kaeskueláan kadi ni Bert ni Lino iti Matemátiks?

6. Ápay a kolkol-apan ni Lino ni Lisa?

7. Ania ti aramíden ni Lisa iti daydiay a Sábado?

8. Ania ti kayat ni Lino nga aramíden?

9. Ania ti kayat ni Lino a buyáen?

10. Ania nga óras ti kayat ni Lino nga ipapanda iti síne?

11. Sinno ti kayat ni Lisa nga ikúyog?

VIII. NOTES

A. Grammar

1. To be specific about which particular thing is being referred to, a demonstrative can be used by itself (as in a. below) or with a following noun (as in b. below):

    a. Basáem daytoy.   Read this.

    b. Basáem daytoy libro.   Read this book.

A demonstrative is also used to distinguish between similar things. In order to do this a linker is placed between the demonstrative and the noun:

c. Basáem daytoy a libro.
Read this book (not the other one).

The full set of demonstratives and their meanings is given in the Glossary.

2. *-EN* VERBS. verbs which have an *-en* suffix are patient focus verbs, i.e., the subject of the sentence is the patient (or object) and not the one doing the action:

a. Buyáenta ti síne   Let's watch the movie.

b. Aláenta ti prútas.   Let's get the fruit.

Notice that the subjects of these sentences *(síne* and *prútas)* are definite, they are translated with the, not a, or some. When either *-ko* or *-mo* are the agent pronouns following an *-en* Verb, the pronoun is joined to the suffix, just like when they follow *-an:*

-en + ko   becomes   -ek
-en + mo   becomes   -em

-an + ko   becomes   -ak
-an + mo   becomes   -am

Compare the following actor focus verbs with their patient focus counterparts. Notice that the difference in English is only in the patient; the patient of an actor-focus verb is indefinite. The patient of a patient-focus verb is definite.

actor-focus   Agbúyaak ti prográma.
                   I'll watch a program.

patient-focus   Buyáek ti prográma.
                   I'll watch the program.

actor-focus   Mangálaak ti prútas.
                   I'll get some fruits.

patient-focus   Aláek ti prútas.
                   I'll get the fruit.

Notice also the different stress patterns on actor-focus and patient-focus verbs. Verbs with an *-an* or *-en* suffix move the stress one syllable closer to the end of the word.

3.

Predicate	Subject	
Noun Verb etc.	ti	Sentence (-Subject)

Kayatmo	ti	agbúya ti síne.
Ania a síne	ti	buyáenta.

Sentences are frequently constructed without any simple noun as the subject. Such sentences contain 'embedded' sentences in place of the noun. These embedded sentences, however, do not contain a subject of their own, e.g., *Kayatmo ti agbúya ti síne?* (Do you want to watch a movie?) In this sentence, *agbúya ti síne* (watch a movie) is an embedded sentence that does not contain a subject.

4. Future Tense. A sentence such as *Agbúyaak ti síne* can have a future meaning as it is (I'll watch a movie). However, it is possible to make it explicitly future by adding a future tense marker, either *-to* (if added to a word ending in a consonant) or *-nto* (if added to a word ending in a vowel):

Agbúyaakto ti síne.	I will watch a movie.
Agbúyakanto ti síne.	You will watch a movie.
Innakto iti malem.	I will go in the afternoon.
Intanto iti malem.	We will go in the afternoon.
Idiayto ti papanak.	Over there is where I'll go.
Ditanto ti papanak.	There is where I'll go.

5. Compound Predicates. In Lesson Five we noticed that certain adverb-like words, such as *pasaray, masansan,* and *kanáyon,* can be joined to a verb with a linker. These form a compound predicate. A number of other words can also

be linked to a verb to form a compound predicate. Two such words are *mabalin* (can) and *masápol* (necessary):

    a. Mabalin a mapanka.   You can go.

    b. Masápol a mapanka.   You must go.

One other commonly occurring compound predicate contains the patient-focus verb *kayat* with a *KO* set pronoun or a genitive noun phrase:

    c. Kayatna a mapanka.   He wants you to go.

    d. Kayat ni Juan a mapanka.   Juan wants you to go.

Notice that in examples c. and d. the agent of *kayat (-na, ni Juan)* and the subject of the sentence *(-ka)* must refer to different people. If they were the same (as in He wants to go), it would be necessary to use an embedded sentence in the subject as described above in section three of these notes:

    e. Kayatna ti mapan.   He wants to go.

A patient-focus verb can also occur in a compound predicate with *kayat* and a *KO* set pronoun or a genitive noun phrase, but the subject of the sentence must refer to another person:

    f. Kayatna a kitáen ni Maria.   He wants to see Maria.

Notice that the agent of *kayat* and *kitáen* may be the same, as in f. above, or it may be different:

    g. Kayatna a kitáek ni Maria.   He wants me to see Maria.

B. Culture

Chaperoning is still commonly practiced in the Philippines, especially in rural areas, and in the city when the family has rural associations. It is customary to have a younger sibling or cousin go along with an elder sister when she is invited out by someone of the opposite sex.

IX. EXERCISES

A. Circle the correct utterance.

1. If Ramona wants Rogelio to look at something and does not specify what it is, what would she say?
   a. Kitáem daytoy.
   b. Kitáem daytoy magasin.
   c. Kitáem daytoy a magasin.

2. If Ramona wants Rogelio to read the newspaper, what would she say?
   a. Basáem daytoy.
   b. Basáem daytoy diario.
   c. Basáem daytoy a diario.

3. If Ramona wants Rogelio to pick a particular mango from the tree, what would she say?
   a. Purusem dayta.
   b. Purusem dayta mangga.
   c. Purusem dayta a mangga.

B. Change the actor-focus sentences into patient-focus. Remember to change the pronoun.

1. Gumátangkami ti karro.   Gatángenmi ti karro. _____

2. Mangálakayo ti danom.   _____

3. Mangantayo ti pinakbet.   _____

4. Bumúlodka man ti lápis.   _____

5. Sumápolka man ti lansa.   _____

6. Mangarámidta ti parol.   _____

7. Agsálaka ti 'Tinikling'.   _____

8. Agkantáka ti 'Mánang Biday'.   _____

9. Agbásaka ti leksionmo.   _____

C. Complete each sentence using the meaning of the final phrase to enable you to decide on the correct form of the verb.

a. ála
- Mangála ni Julio _____ ti sábong. _____
  Julio will get / a/some flower(s).
- Aláen ni Julio _____ ti sábong. _____
  Julio will get / the flower.

b. dáwat
- _____ ti papel. _____
  My Áding will ask for / a piece of/some paper(s).
- _____ ti papel. _____
  My Áding will ask for / the paper.

c. sápol
- _____ ti lansa. _____
  Telma will look for / a/some nail(s).
- _____ ti lansa. _____
  Telma will look for / the nail.

d. kan
- _____ ti saba. _____
  I will eat / a/some banana(s).
- _____ ti saba. _____
  I will eat / the banana.

e. kanta
- _____ ti kundíman. _____
  You sing / a love song.
- _____ ti 'Bannatíran' _____
  You sing / 'Bannatiran'.

f. sála
- _____ ti ballet. _____
  Let's dance / ballet.
- _____ ti 'Swan Lake'. _____
  Let's dance / 'Swan Lake'.

D. List five things that you would like to do today.

1. Kayatko ti mangan ti hálu-hálo.

2. _____

3. _____

4. _____

5. _____

6. _____

E. You just bought a 'Bannawag', a ripe banana, a fish, a Coke, some pictures, and a newspaper. Say what you want to do with these objects.

   1. Kayatko a basáen ti Bannáwag.

   2. _____

   3. _____

   4. _____

   5. _____

   6. _____

F. Write the correct form of the future tense marker in the blank spaces.

'Ti Padayámi'	'Our Party'
Intuno Sábado, ad-ad_____padayámi. Ado_____ti makan ken mainom idiay.	On Saturday, we will have a party. There will be a lot of food and drink.
Aglúto_____ni Leah ti pinakbet. Agarámid_____ni Esteban ti lumpia. Mangitu-'got_____ ni Tessie ti ser-	Leah will cook *pinakbet*. Esteban will make *lumpia*. Tessie will bring some beer and San Miguel gin. Also, Lucas will buy some hors

98

bésa ken Hiniebra San Miguel. Gumátang_____ met ni Lucas ti pulútan. Siak, agapóyak _____.

d'oeurves. As for me, I'll cook rice.

Agkanta_____ni Yolanda ken aggitára _____ni Lito. Bumúlod-_____ni Susana ti 'projector' ta agbúyakami_____ ti 'slide'.

Yolanda will sing, and Lito will play guitar. Susana will borrow a projector because we will look at some slides.

Idiay_____balay da Maria ti pagdayaanmi ta dakkel ti balayda.

Our party will be at Maria's place, because their house is big.

Naragsak_____únay ti padayámi!

Our party will be a lot of fun!

G. Each of you will participate in creating a dialog on the board, every sentence of which must contain either *kayat* or *diak kayat* with either an actor-focus or an object-focus verb:

A: Kayatmo ti mangan?

B: Saan, diak kayat ti mangan.

A: Ania ngarod ti kayatmo nga aramíden?

B: Kayatko a basáen daytoy librok.

A: Ay, kayatko ti mangan, sa matúrog, ta nabannógak únay.

B: Ala ngarod, ta la kaykayatmo nga aramíden.
(ken daddúma pay)

Your teacher will help you correct the errors and explain them to you.

X. COMMUNICATION ACTIVITY

A. You are Bert's real estate agent and have several houses to sell. You call Bert's friend and ask her if she would like to look at a beautiful house you are selling. At first, she refuses and gives her reason, but you convince her. She asks what kind of house it is. You describe it to her and then she agrees to go with you in order to see it. She really likes the house but does not have enough money for a down payment. Work it out so that she is able to buy the house in spite of her financial difficulty.

B. The phone rings and it is your friend who has just bought a new car. He no longer likes the car and he would like to sell it to you. You are interested in it but you are wondering why he is selling it. You try to find out why and won't stop until you are satisfied with the answer.

C. Study the following vocabulary thoroughly in preparation for the game that follows.

agdiram-os	wash face
agsagaysay	comb hair
agdígos	take a bath
aggulgol	shampoo hair
agsipilio	brush teeth
agmeykap	apply makeup
agsapátos	put on shoes
agbádo	put on clothes
agpantalon	put on pants
agkallugong	put on a hat
aglagto	jump
agtugaw	sit
agwatwat	exercise
agsála	dance
agbása	read
agsúrat	write
agbílang	count
umísem	smile

uminom	drink
mangan	eat
matúrog	sleep

Game: Kuna ni Kulas (Kulas Says)

Rules:

1. Form a circle and choose a leader.
2. The leader will give commands. If his command is preceded by *'Kuna ni Kulas'*, the player will execute the command.
3. If the command is not preceded by *'Kuna ni Kulas'*, the players will remain stationary.
4. Players will be disqualified if they perform a command incorrectly, or perform a command which is not preceded by *'Kuna ni Kulas'*.

For example:

"Kuna ni Kulas . . . 'Aglagtótayo' "

Everybody says "Aglagtótayo," then jumps.

XI.   WRITING PRACTICE

A. Analyze and explain A's request in the last utterance of the dialog.

B. Write a short anecdote based on a chaperoning experience.

Lesson Eight

I. DIALOG: Visiting Friends

Study the following dialog. Try to understand the meaning of each sentence by referring to the literal translations in the box.

1

1. A: Adda táo, Ápo!

2. B: Sumrekka. . . .
   Ay, Caridad, sika
   gáyam!

2

3. A: Ania ti ar-aramí-
   denyo?

4. B: Mangmangankami
   ti mangga.

3

5. A: Mangmangankayo
   ti naáta
   a mangga?

6. C: Wen, naímas daytoy.
   Ne, manganka.
   Ramanam.

4

7. A: Diak kayat ti naáta
   a mangga. Naalsem
   únay.

8. C: Saan únay a naalsem
   daytoy.

9. A: Ramanak man
   ngarod. Bassit
   láeng.

adda	there-is
táo	person
Ápo	sir
sumrekka	enter-you
sika	you
gáyam	so
ania	what
ar-aramídenyo	doing-you
mangmangankami	eating-we
mangga	mango
mangmangankayo	eating-you (plural)
naáta	green, unripe
naímas	tasty
daytoy	this
manganka	eat-you
ramanam	taste-you
diak	negative-I
kayat	like
naalsem	sour
únay	very
saan	negative
ramanak	taste-I
man	please
bassit	little, few
láeng	only
ne	here
buggúong	fermented-fish-sauce (bagoong)
ngem	but
mangálaka	get-you
pay	more

102

5

10. B: Ne, ramanam.
Kayatmo ti
buggúong?

11. A: Wen, kayatko, ngem
bassit láeng.
Ay, naímas gáyam
ti naáta a
mangga ken
buggúong!

12. C: Ne, mangálaka pay.

II. TRANSLATING THE DIALOG

Write a free translation of the dialog (i.e., a translation in natural
English). Do it in pencil, and then check it against the translation in
Appendix One. Make whatever corrections are necessary.

A:_____

B:_____

A:_____

B:_____

A:_____

C:_____

A:_____

C:_____

A:_____

B:_____

A:_____

C:_____

III.   LEARNING THE DIALOG

After the presentation of the dialog, let one of you volunteer to be a learner and go to the front of the class. Help that person memorize the dialog, then call for another volunteer learner. Afterwards, three of you will say the dialog to one another.

IV.   ROLE-PLAYING

How would you say the dialog in the situations below?

A.   A visit B and C at the dormitory. As she walks into the room she is surprised to see them grimacing.

B.   A is passing by and sees B and C sitting on the stairs.

C.   A opens the door and sees B and C eating green mangoes. C's mother is sleeping nearby.

V.   VOCABULARY

Familiarize yourself with the following words which you will need to use in the following sections. Ask your teacher to help you pronounce them correctly.

A. Nouns

adóbo	meat dish with spices and vinegar
asin	salt
bádo	clothes
basúra	trash, garbage
bir	beer
biskwit	crackers
kálog	young coconut
dulse	candy
gátas	milk
bayábas	guava
itlog	egg
itsa	tea
kape	coffee
karne	meat
késo	cheese

mani	peanuts
niog	coconut
paria	bittermelon
patis	fish sauce
saba	banana
serbésa	beer
síli	pepper
sorbéte	ice cream
suka	vinegar
tsampoy	salted seeds

B. Verbs (continuative or customary)

1. AG-

agad-ádal	studying
agal-ála	getting, gathering
agbasbása	reading
agar-arámid	making
agbuybúya	watching, viewing
agdádáit	sewing
agdaldalos	cleaning
agin-inana	resting
agkankanta	singing
aglutlúto	cooking
agpurpuros	picking
agpidpídot	picking up
agsalsála	dancing
agsursúrat	writing
agtrabtrabáho	working
agtugtugaw	sitting
agwatwatwat	exercising

2. -UM-

umin-inom	drinking

3. -EN

ad-adálen	studying
al-aláen	getting, gathering
ar-aramíden	doing, making
basbasáen	reading
buybuyáen	viewing, watching
dádaíten	sewing
dawdawáten	asking for
dengdenggen	listening to
in-inumen	drinking
kankanen	eating
makmakiniliáen	typing
pidpidúten	picking up
purpurusen	picking (fruit)
salsaláen	dancing
salsaludsúden	asking (a question)
sapsapúlen	looking for
sursuráten	writing
toktokaren	playing (an instrument)

C. Adjectives

naalsem	sour
naapgad	salty
nagásang	spicy
napait	bitter
nasam-it	sweet
nasugpet	puckery, tart
naáta	green, unripe
naganos	tender
nakulbet	tough, chewy
nalamíis	cold
nalukneng	soft

naluom	ripe
napúdot	hot, warm
narugit	dirty
narúnaw	melted
natangken	hard

VI. CHANGING THE DIALOG

A. Using the situations below, and referring to the vocabulary section that you have just studied, how would you change:

PART 1 of the dialog?

1. B asks A to come in, offers a seat, a snack and a drink of Coke.

2. B asks A to come up and eat.

3. B looks very tired so A suggests that she rest.

PART 2 of the dialog?

1. B and C are
- cooking.
- exercising.
- having a snack.
- resting.
- reading.
- working.
- writing.
- singing.
- studying.
- cleaning.

2. B and C are
- eating young coconuts.
- sewing clothes for themselves.
- picking mangoes.
- picking flowers.
- picking up trash.
- drinking Coke.
- eating hot peppers.
- watching TV.

3. A wants to know what B and C are

- eating.
- reading.
- sewing.
- studying.
- watching.
- collecting, getting, gathering.
- making.
- singing.
- dancing.
- listening to.
- playing (music).
- writing.
- drinking.
- picking.
- picking up.
- looking for.
- asking for.
- typing.

PART 3 of the dialog?

1. B and C are eating

- spicy-hot adobo.
- sour guavas.
- green bananas.
- tough meat.
- melted ice cream.

2. B and C are drinking

- hot milk.
- cold tea.
- bitter coffee.

PART 4 of the dialog?

1. A doesn't like

- candy because it's very sweet.
- a lot of curry because it's very hot.
- green bananas because they are very puckery.
- salted seeds because they are very salty.
- bittermelon because it is very bitter.
- very ripe bananas because they are too soft.

PART 5 of the dialog?

1. A offers B some $\left\{\begin{array}{l}\text{salt}\\\text{patis}\\\text{vinegar}\end{array}\right\}$ with green mango.

2. A offers B some $\left\{\begin{array}{l}\text{cheese}\\\text{peanuts}\\\text{crackers}\end{array}\right\}$ with cold beer.

B. How would you change the dialog in the situations below?

1. A asks what B and C are reading, instead of what they are doing.

2. Only B is eating mangoes. C is doing something else.

3. A is the resident manager of the dorm. He is fifty years old.

4. A does not like mango with bagoong, and politely says so in a roundabout way. She also politely refuses to take more mango and offers an excuse for her refusal.

VII. QUESTION AND ANSWER

Get a partner and practice asking and answering these questions with him or her. Try asking other questions, too. Ask your teacher to give you the Ilokano for words you do not know. Speak only in Ilokano.

1. Sinno ti simmangpet?

2. Ania ti ar-aramíden da B ken C?

3. Ania a kláse ti mangga ti kankanen da B ken C?

4. Apay a saan a kayat ni A ti naáta a mangga?

5. Rinamanan kadi ni A ti naáta a mangga?

6. Ania pay ti kinnanda?

7. Ania ti nangisawsáwanda iti mangga?

8. Nagustuan kadi ni A ti naáta a mangga ken buggúong?

9. Magustuanyo kadi ti naáta a mangga ken buggúong?

10. Ania dagiti kanen a saanyo a magustuan?

11. Ania dagiti kanen a naalsem únay?

VIII.   NOTES

A. Grammar

1. Negative Auxiliary. There are two negative words in Ilokano, *saan* and *di*. Although there are some sentences in which either form can be used, there are others in which only one of the negatives can be appropriately used.

One of the main differences between *saan* and *di* is that *saan* acts like a verb in that it is necessary to have a linker between it and a following sentence which it negates:

Saan nga agtrabtrabáho Ni Juan.	Juan is not working.
Saan nga áso dayta.	That is not a dog.
Saan a nabsog ni Carmen.	Carmen is not full.

On the other hand *di* is an auxiliary, like *mapan* and *umay* because it does not need a linker between itself and a following verb:

Di nagsao ti lakay.	The old man did not speak.

Another difference between *saan* and *di* is that *saan* can be used as a negative with any sentence (except existentials, which use *awan*), whereas *di* is much more restricted as a negator. It can be used with most if not all verbs, but generally not with adjectives and nouns. *Di* can be used with some adjectives and nouns as long as it is separated from the negativized word by a pronoun and/or one or more sentence modifiers. Even with verbs, *di* seems to be used rather than *saan* more often when there are modifiers between *di* and the verb:

Di nagtrabáho ni Juan.	Juan did not work.
Di kano met nagtrabáho ni Juan.	Juan did not work (as expected), they say.

110

Di met nasingpet dayta nga ubing.	That child is not nice.
(*Di nasingpet dayta nga ubing).	(contrary to expectation).
Di met gáyam maestro ti kaarrúbatayo.	So, our neighbor is not a teacher.
(*Di maestro ti kaarrúbatayo.)	Our neighbor is not a teacher.

A further difference between *saan* and *di* is in the form of the pronoun which is used for the genitive first person singular (I). The regular form *-ko* is attached to *saan,* however, *-ak* is used with *di:*

Saanko a kinnan ti mansánas.	I didn't eat the apples.
Diak kinnan ti mansánas.	

When the genitive second person pronoun is attached to *di,* it is irregular. Usually, following vowels, *-mo* is shortened to *-m.* When it follows *di,* however, the full form is used:

Dímo kadi inan-ano ti ubing?	Didn't you do anything
(*Dim kadi inan-ano ti ubing?)	to the child?

2. *-AN* Verbs. Verbs which have an *-an* suffix are patient-focus verbs, just like *-EN* verbs. The subject of the sentence is the patient. Most verbs, when they are patient-focus, have either *-en* or *-an* as the suffix, although there are some that can have either. Most verbs that take *-an* are those where the patient is only partly affected by the action, or it is only the surface which is affected. Most cleaning verbs take an *-an* suffix:

innáwan	wash
labaan	launder
dalusan	clean
sagádan	sweep
etc.	

3. Many words in Ilokano have double consonants in the middle, such as *serrek* (enter), *kelleb* (to lie on the stomach), and *bettak* (explode).

When *-um-* is inserted into these words, the first vowel and the first of the double consonants are dropped:

sumrek	to enter
kumleb	to lie on one's stomach
bumtak	to explode

4. Sentence Modifiers.

    a. *láeng* just, only. This modifier is sometimes abbreviated to *la,* especially when joined to the word for like—*kas:*

        kasla táo   just like a person

    b. *man* please. This modifier is commonly used whenever a request is made. It makes the request more polite, like please does in English. There are many sentences, however, where *man* is used where it does not mean please.

    c. *pay* still, moreover, yet. This modifier has approximately the opposite meaning to *-en* (now, already, not anymore). Often, if one of the two appears in a question, the other one appears in the answer:

        Q: Nangankan?   Did you eat already?
        A: Saan pay.   Not yet.

        Q: Nanganka pay?   Did you eat some more?
        A: Saánen.   No.

5. Adjectives. In Lesson Three we noted that many adjectives are formed by prefixing *na-* to the root word:

nasayáat	fine
nagaget	industrious
naimbag	good

There are, however, many adjectives which do not have any affixes at all. Some of these begin with *a,* which is an old adjective-forming prefix which is no longer used as a prefix and just forms part of the root word:

ababa	short
asideg	near

adayo	far
atiddog	long
akába	wide
akíkid	narrow
etc.	

A number of adjectives are simply root words:

dakkel	big
bassit	small
dáan	old
baro	new
etc.	

Other adjectives are formed with a *ma-* prefix:

mabisin	hungry
mabain	shy
mabuteng	afraid
masakit	sick

6. In Lesson Six, we learned about CVC-reduplication, and some of its meanings. We noted how with actor-focus verbs it gives either a. continuative or b. customary meaning. The same meanings occur when CVC- is used on patient-focus verbs:

a. Dádaítenna ti bádona.
   She is sewing her dress.

b. Kanáyon a basbasáenna dagiti súratmo.
   He is always reading your letters.

A verb is continuative when the action is on-going, whether in the present or in the past, and customary when the action is done on a recurring basis.

B. Culture

When announcing one's self as a visitor, it is not normal to knock on the door of an Ilokano home. It is usual to call, *Adda táo, Ápo!* Literally: There is a person, Sir! The response from within is usually *Sumrekka* (Come in) or *Umúlika* (Come up). In traditional Ilokano society, the latter would be most commonly used because houses are set on poles, and access to the house is up the house ladder called *agdan*.

IX. EXERCISES

A. Write the continuative forms of the following verbs. The underlined portion is the root word.

aglúto	Aglutlúto	ni Juan ita. Juan is cooking now.
aglaba		ti ubing idiay banio. The child is washing clothes in the bathroom.
aginana		I'm resting.
agádal		kayo, ania? You (plural) are studying, aren't you?
mangála		ni Nita ti sábong. Nita is getting some flowers.
mangarámid		ni Nána ti kagay. Nána is making a shawl.
kitáen	Kitkitáen	da ti babái. They are looking at the woman.
saludsúden		ni Fely ni Lorna. Fely is asking Lorna a question.
ikkaten		dagiti lalláki ti lansa. The men are removing the nail.
iwáen		ni Felix ti karne. Felix is slicing the meat.

B. Complete the following dialog by providing responses that contain continuative forms of the following verbs.

ay-áyam	tugaw
dáit	inana
bása	súrat
búya	dalos
sála	ádal

114

Abraham:	Helo!
Moises:	Ania ti ar-aramídenyo, dita?
Abraham:	Agay-ay-áyam ni Jesus.
Moises:	Ket ni Nána Magdalena, ania ti ar-aramídenna?
Abraham:	_____
Moises:	Ania met ti ar-aramíden da Maria ken Jose?
Abraham:	_____
Moises:	Agad-ádal ni Mateo?
Abraham:	Saan,_____
Moises:	Ayan ni Marcos, ngay?
Abraham:	_____
Moises:	Adda ni Táta Pablo?
Abraham:	Wen,_____
Moises:	Ania met ti ar-aramíden ni Lazaro?
Abraham:	_____
Moises:	Ket ni Salome, ngay?
Abraham:	_____
Moises:	Ket sika, ania ti ar-aramídem?
Abraham:	_____

C. What questions would Ana be likely to ask in the following situations?

1. She sees Jose watching TV.

   Ania ti buybuyáen ni Jose?

2. She sees Emy eating.

---

3. She sees Gloria reading.

_____

4. She sees Jessie writing.

_____

5. She hears Ed playing the piano.

_____

6. She hears Andres singing.

_____

7. She sees Fernando dancing.

_____

8. She sees Juanito sewing.

_____

9. She sees Belen making something.

_____

10. She sees Alma listening to a song.

_____

11. She sees Evelyn looking at something.

_____

12. She sees Tessie looking for something.

_____

D. Change the following *saan* sentences to *di*.

1. Saanka kadi nga   Díka kadi agtrabáho?
   agtrabáho?

2. Saának a mapan.   Diak mapan.

3. Saanko a kayat ti mapan. _____

4. Ápay a saanmo a kayat ti
   agpasiar? _____

5. Saanna a daíten ti bádok. _____

6. Saanna a kayat a basáen ti
   leksionna. _____

7. Sinno ti saanda nga
   awísen? _____

8. Ania ti saantayo a
   buyáen? _____

9. Saanmonto a kanen dayta. _____

10. Saantanto nga ibaga
    kenkuána. _____

E. You have several chores to do at home. List them, using -An
   patient-focus verbs.

1. Punásak ti lamisáan.   I will wipe the table.

2. _____

3. _____

4. _____

5. _____

6. _____

X.   COMMUNICATION ACTIVITY

A. Fill out the sheet and then find out who was in the same place
   doing the same thing at the same time as yourself.

Nágan   Ayan mo iti . . .   Addáak. . . Ania ti ar-aramídem?
Name   where were you . . I was . . .   What were you doing?

117

_____ 7:00 P.M.? _____ _____

_____ 8:45 A.M.? _____ _____

_____ 9:00 P.M.? _____ _____

_____ 10:15 P.M.? _____ _____

_____ 11:40 A.M.? _____ _____

_____ 12:00 noon? _____ _____

_____ 1:30 P.M.? _____ _____

_____ 2:00 P.M.? _____ _____

_____ 3:25 P.M.? _____ _____

_____ 4:00 P.M.? _____ _____

_____ 5:20 P.M.? _____ _____

_____ 6:00 P.M.? _____ _____

_____ 7:05 P.M.? _____ _____

_____ 8:00 P.M.? _____ _____

_____ 9:35 P.M.? _____ _____

_____ 10:00 P.M.? _____ _____

B. Describe each of the nouns in the right hand column using one or more of the adjectives in the left hand column. The nouns can be described positively, e.g., *Nasam-it ti dulse* (Candies are sweet), or negatively, e.g., *Saan a nasam-it ti paria* (Bittermelon is not sweet).

nangína	expensive	balay	house
nalaka	cheap	ngílaw	fly
		ípes	cockroach
mayat	nice, good	bato	stone

118

madi	not good	káyo	tree
		apoy	fire
dakkel	big	yélo	ice
bassit	small	túdo	rain
		init	sun
natangken	hard	tiempo	weather
nalukneng	soft	rosas	rose
		posporo	matches
naímas	delicious	karro	car
		bisikléta	bicycle
nabangsit	odorous	eropláno	airplane
nabanglo	fragrant	papel	paper
		kutson	mattress
adayo	far	Porsche	
asideg	near	Mercedes Benz	
		"Funny Girl"	
napuskol	thick	"Star Wars"	
naingpis	thin		
		Tsina	
napintas	beautiful	Pilipinas	
naalas	ugly	Molokai	
		Lanai	
natáyag	tall		
pandek/ababa	short	Raquel Welch	
		Wilt Chamberlain	
napúdot	hot	Twiggy	
nalamíis	cold, cool	Rockefeller	
nalukmeg	fat	Matematiks	
nakuttong	skinny		
		naluom a saba	ripe banana
napigsa	strong	naáta a mangga	green mango
nakapsot	weak	nalungsot a prútas	rotten fruit

narugit	dirty	nabaknang	rich
nadalos	clean	napobre	poor
narígat	difficult	naalsem	sour
nalaka	easy	nasam-it	sweet

C.

A

You are eating lunch with B. You are trying to get her to taste one of your favorite foods, bagoong.

B

You refuse to taste the food that A wants you to taste because to you, it looks awful and it's smelly.

Goal: To get B to taste it.

D. Collect pictures of people doing different things. Describe your pictures to the class.

E. Show a picture to the class. Ask your classmates to describe what is in the picture and what's happening.

XI. WRITING PRACTICE

A. The class will divide into two groups, each of which will create its own dialog on the board. Each member of a group will provide one sentence toward the formation of the dialog. Group 1 must have the negatives *di* or *saan* in each sentence. Group 2 must utilize either one of the sentence modifiers *-en* or *pay* in their sentences. (See Lesson Seven for example.)

B. Get a partner and together create a continuation of the dialog by adding three or more coherent exchanges to it. Be creative.

Lesson Nine

I.   DIALOG: A Relative Arrives

Study the following dialog. Try to understand the meaning of each
sentence by referring to the literal translations in the box.

1

1. A: Ay, Ápo makaturtúro-
       gak!

2. B: Ápay, díka kadi
       nakatúrog
       idi rabii?

3. A: Natúrogak ngem
       bassit laeng, ta
       napanmi sinábat ti
       uliteg ni Burcio itay
       parbángon.

2

4. B: Ápay, naggapuanna?

5. A: Naggapo idiay Pili-
       pínas.
       Alas trésen idi
       simmangpet.
       Idi kuan,
       napankami idiay
       balayda.

3

6. B: Ania ti inarámidyo
       idiay?

7. A: Nangankami ti balot
       sa imminomkami ti
       serbésa.
       Nagado ti kinnan-
       ko a balot!

makaturtúrogak	feel sleepy-I
ápay	why
díka	not-you
kadi	question marker
nakatúrog	was able to sleep
natúrog	slept
idi	remote past
napanmi	went-we (exclusive)
sinábat	met
uliteg	uncle
itay	recent past
parbángon	dawn
naggapuanna	place-came from-he
naggapo	came from
simmangpet	arrived
idi kuan	later on (idiom)
kua	whatchamacallit
balayda	house-their
inarámidyo	did-you
nangankami	ate-we
balot	boiled unhatched duck egg
sa	then (sequence)
imminomkami	drank-we
serbésa	beer
nagado	so much
kinnanko	ate-I
dímo	negative-you
aya	tag question
wen, a	of course (idiom)
mandiak	not-like-I
nagalas	so ugly

121

4

8. B: Mano ti kinnanmo?

9. A: Pito.

10. B: Pito! Apay, mang-
    manganka ti balot,
    aya?

11. A: Wen, a! Ápay, dímo
    kayat ti balot?

12. B: Mandiak! Nagalas!

II.   TRANSLATING THE DIALOG

Write a free translation of the dialog (i.e., a translation in natural
English). Do it in pencil, and then check it against the translation in
Appendix One. Make whatever corrections are necessary.

A:_____

B:_____

A:_____

B:_____

A:_____

B:_____

A:_____

B:_____

A:_____

B:_____

A:_____

B:_____

III.   LEARNING THE DIALOG

   After the presentation of the dialog, take a partner and practice
   with him or her. Afterward, your teacher will call two people from
   the class to say the dialog to each other.

IV.   ROLE-PLAYING

   How would you say the dialog in the situations below?

   A. A keeps yawning. Her eyelids look very heavy. She moves slug-
      gishly.

   B. A and B are in class. The teacher is lecturing and keeps looking
      at them. They look guilty but can't stop talking.

   C. B has mild laryngitis.

   D. B is hard of hearing.

V.   VOCABULARY

   Familiarize yourself with the following words that you will need to
   use in changing the dialog. Ask your teacher to help you pronounce
   them correctly.

   A. Nouns

ábal-ábal	beetles
áso	dog
bási	sugar cane wine
bisukol	snail
dára	blood
datar	floor
dúdon	locust
kabalio	horse
karne	meat
nuang	carabao
úleg	snake
yo	shark

B. Verbs

1. AG- (continuative or customary)

agkamkammet	eating with the hands
agsigsigarilio	smoking

(past tense NAG-)

naginom	drank liquor
nagsála	danced
nagwatwat	exercised
nagádal	studied
nagmerienda	had a snack
nagpasiar	took a stroll

2. MANG- (past tense NANG-)

nangan	ate
nangála	got, took

3. -UM- (past tense -IM- or -IMM-)

bumílang/ bimmílang	count/counted
bumúlod/ bimmúlod	borrow/borrowed
gumátang/ gimmátang	buy/bought

4. -EN (past tense -IN-)

binása	read
binílang	counted
binúlod	borrowed
ginátang	bought
inarámid	made, did
ininom	drank
innála	got, took
kinanta	sang
kinnan	ate
linúto	cooked
minerienda	snacked on

| pinatay | killed, turned off |
| pinídot | picked up |

5. PAG—AN (past tense NAG—AN)
   PANG—AN (past tense NANG—AN)

nagsaláan	place where (one) danced
nagpasiáran	place where (one) took a stroll
nagwatwátan	place where (one) exercised
nagadálan	place where (one) studied
nagmeriendáan	place where (one) took a snack
nanganan	place where (one) ate some
nangaláan	place where (one) got some

6. MA- (past tense NA-)

maúlaw	to feel dizzy
mauwaw	to be thirsty
mabsog	to be full

C. MA- (adjectives)

| mabisin | hungry |

VI. CHANGING THE DIALOG

A. Using the situations below, and referring to the vocabulary section that you have just studied, how would you change:

PART 1 of the dialog?

1. A is
   - hungry.
   - tired.
   - thirsty.
   - dizzy.

PART 2 of the dialog?

1. They went to meet Burcio's
   - aunt.
   - mother.
   - father.
   - grandmother.
   - sister-in-law.
   - brother-in-law.
   - niece.

2. Burcio's relative
   arrived from

   { Japan.
   China.
   Europe.
   Samoa.
   Chicago.

3. He arrived at

   { 5:30 P.M.
   4:00 P.M.
   2:45 P.M.
   12:00 M. (noon)
   1:15 P.M.
   7:50 P.M.

4. B asked A
   where they

   { danced.
   took a stroll.
   exercised.
   studied.
   had a snack.
   got some mangoes.
   ate.

PART 3 of the dialog?

1. B asks what
   they

   { ate.
   picked.
   made.
   watched on TV.
   read.
   took.
   borrowed.
   bought.
   sang.
   picked up.
   drank.
   cooked.
   counted.
   snacked on.

126

PART 4 of the dialog?

1. B asks dis-
   believingly
   if A eats
   $\begin{cases} \text{locusts.} \\ \text{beetles.} \\ \text{snails.} \\ \text{snakes.} \\ \text{dog meat.} \\ \text{horse meat.} \\ \text{carabao meat.} \\ \text{blood.} \\ \text{shark.} \end{cases}$

2. B asks if A
   $\begin{cases} \text{eats with her hands.} \\ \text{smokes.} \\ \text{sleeps on the floor.} \\ \text{drinks sugar cane wine.} \end{cases}$

B. How would you change the dialog in the situations below?

1. A is very hungry. She has just come from a long meeting.

2. B is A's uncle.

3. A went to a party of a friend the night before. They ate a lot and did many things at the party.

4. Burcio's uncle came from Japan. He arrived at midnight. They went to a bar for a drink afterwards.

5. A is B's neighbor. B is a teacher.

VII. QUESTION AND ANSWER

Get a partner and practice asking and answering the questions with him or her. Try asking other questions, too. Ask your teacher to give you the Ilokano for words you do not know. Speak only in Ilokano.

1. Sinno ti makaturtúrog?

2. Ápay a saan a nakatúrog ni B iti napalábas a rabii?

3. Naggapuan ti uliteg ni Burcio?

4. Ania nga óras idi simmangpet ti uliteg ni Burcio?

5. Sadinno pay ti napanan da A?

6. Ania ti inarámid da A idiay balay ti uliteg ni Burcio?

7. Mano ti kinnan ni A nga balot?

8. Kayat kadi ni A ti balot?

9. Ápay a dína kayat ni B ti balot?

10. Ket sika, kayatmo ti balot? Ápay?

11. Ania dagiti dímo kayat a kanen?

VIII. NOTES

A. Grammar

1. Past Tense of Verbs. In Ilokano, when a verb is in the past tense, it means the action was completed some time in the past.

There are several different ways to make verbs past tense.

a. Those which have prefixes *ag-, mang-,* and *ma-* begin with *n-* in the following way:

noncompleted	completed
aglagto	naglagto
mangan	nangan
mapan	napan

b. *-um-* becomes *-im-* or *-imm-*. If the verb is like *sumrek,* in which *-um-* is immediately followed by a consonant (in this case, *r*), *-im-* is used. If *-um-* is followed by a vowel, *-imm* is used:

noncompleted	completed
sumrek	simrek
bumtak	bimtak
uminom	imminom
umúli	immúli

c. Patient-focus verbs with *-en* or *-an* suffixes have an *-in-* inserted before the first vowel. If the suffix is *-en,* only *-in-* appears; *-en* is removed. If the suffix is *-an,* *-in-* and *-an* both appear:

noncompleted	completed
basáen lutuen inumen	binása linúto ininom
sagádan diram-úsan innáwan	sinagádan diniram-úsan ininnáwan

There are two common patient focus verbs taking *-en* as their noncompleted affix that have an irregular past tense. These are *aláen* (to get) and *kanen* (to eat). Instead of *-in-*, *-inn-* must be inserted:

noncompleted	completed
aláen kanen	innála kinnan

d. A locative gerund like *pagtrabahuan,* can be made past tense by changing *pag-* to *nag-:*

noncompleted	completed
pagtrabahuan paggapuan paglabaan papanan paggianan	nagtrabahuan naggapuan naglabaan napanan naggianan

2. Intensive Adjectives. It is possible to make an intensive adjective by using *únay* (very):

Napintas únay ni Maria.   Maria is very pretty.

Dakkel únay ti balayda.   Their house is very big.

An intensive adjective can also be formed by using *nag-* instead of *na-* as the prefix that forms the adjective:

Nagpintas ni Maria.   Maria is very beautiful.

Nagdakkel ti balayda.   Their house is very big.

Nagado ti kinnanko!   I ate so much!

A third way of forming an intensive adjective in Ilokano is to reduplicate the root word with CVC-, then prefix it with *naka-:*

nakadakdakkel	very big
nakaad-ado	very many
nakapinpintas	very beautiful

IX.   EXERCISES

A. Write the past tense form of each verb or gerund in the blanks in the following sentences.

1. Sadinno ti nagtrabahuam idi tawen?
   pagtrabahuam
   where did you work last year?

2. Ania ti _____ idiay kusína?
   aláem
   What did you get from the kitchen?

3. Ado ti _____ a mani idi rabii.
   kanek
   I ate a lot of peanuts last night.

4. _____ idiay Kalihi idi búlan?
   Paggianam
   Where did you stay in Kalihi last month?

5. _____ ni Crising idi kalman?
   Papanan
   Where did Crising go yesterday?

6. Ania ti _____ ni David iti tíbi?
   buyáen
   What did David watch on TV?

7. Idiay eskuéla ti _____ itay.
   paggapuak
   I came from the school a while ago.

8. Sinno ti _____ iti míting idi láwasna?
     mapan
   Who went to the meeting last week?

9. Sinno ti _____ ti pamigat?
     aglúto
   Who cooked the breakfast?

10. Dakami ti _____ ti sábong itay malem.
      mangála
    We were the ones who got the flowers this afternoon.

11. _____ idiay baybay itay.
      Aggapó-ak
    I came from the beach a while ago.

12. Sinno ti _____ ti tinápay?
      gumátang
    Who bought the bread?

13. Ania ti _____ ni Matilda idi láwasna?
      aramíden
    What did Matilda do last week?

B. Write the past tense form of the verb indicated in each blank in
   the following story. If you do not know the verb, you can find
   its basic form in the glossary.

   _____ ni Laura iti   Laura arrived at six
     arrived   o'clock. She came
                                     from work. She went
   alas sais. _____ iti   up to their house, sat
     came from   down, and read the
                                     newspaper. Laura
   trabáhona. _____ iti   rested for five min-
     went up   utes. She drank some
                                     milk.
   balayda, _____, sána
     sat down

   _____ ti diario.
     read

131

_____ iti lima a minúto.
rested

_____ ti gátas.
drank

_____ ni Laura idiay
went
kusína. _____ ti
cooked
pangrabiína, sa _____.
ate

_____ -na ti pingganna,
washed

sána _____.
wiped

Iti alas dies, _____
took a bath

_____, _____ -na ti
brushed teeth   turned off
sílaw, sa _____. Nalukneng
went to sleep
ti katre a _____ -na.
slept on

Laura went to the kitchen, cooked her dinner, and then ate. She washed her dishes and dried them.

At ten o'clock, she took a bath, brushed her teeth, turned off the light and went to sleep. The bed she slept on was soft.

C. List five things you did not do last week. Use each of the verb forms for each of your sentences, but use different verbs. Translate your sentences into English.

1. Diak inádal ti leksionko iti Ilokano.

2. Saának a napan idiay simbáan.

3. Saanko a dinalusan ti kuartok.

4. Saának a nagbúya ti síne.

5. Diak nangan ti prútas.

6. (-en) _____

132

7. (ma-) _____

8. (-in--an) _____

9. (ag-) _____

10. (mang-) _____

D. Rewrite the following sentences using the three different intensive forms of the adjective.

Bassit ti tugaw.   The chair is small.

    1. Bassit únay ti tugaw!

    2. Nagbassit ti tugaw!

    3. Nakabasbassit ti tugaw!

Naalas ti tiempo.   The weather is bad.

    1. Naalas únay ti tiempo!

    2. Nagalas ti tiempo!

    3. Nakaal-alas ti tiempo!

Adayo ti Australia.

    1. _____

    2. _____

    3. _____

Atiddog daytoy tali.

    1. _____

    2. _____

    3. _____

Nangísit ti lángit ita.

    1. _____

2._____

3._____

Ado ti táo ditoy paggígianam.

    1._____

    2._____

    3._____

Naánoska.

    1._____

    2._____

    3._____

Nalaing (isúna).

    1._____

    2._____

    3._____

E. Using any of the adjective intensifiers, what would you say if you:

    1. were very impressed with Dr. Dominggo?

       _____!

    2. were very mad at Elisa?

       _____!

    3. liked the food a lot?

       _____!

    4. were one in a family of ten and you were given a one-bedroom house?

       _____!

5. were describing a 50-room castle where you stayed in Europe?

_____!

6. walked into a party and saw five long tables filled with food?

_____!

X.   COMMUNICATION ACTIVITY

   A. Complete the partial sentence that your teacher will read to you. The teacher will complete the sentence with an appropriate noun and keep it a secret. You have ten chances to guess the noun the teacher is thinking of.

      1. Basbasáen ni Norma ti_____

      2. Bilbilángen ni Lorna ti_____

      3. Aglutlúto ni Irma ti_____

      4. Agbuybúya dagiti estudiante ti_____

      5. Mapmapan ni Ádingko idiay_____

      6. Matmatúrog da Tessie idiay_____

      7. Nagado ti inarámidko a_____

      8. Nagado ti kinnanko a_____

      9. Bassit ti ginátangko a_____

     10. Bassit ti innálak a_____

   B. Write a response to the question that your teacher will read to you. The teacher will choose one response and keep it a secret. You have ten chances to guess the response.

      1. A: Kumustáka?

         B: _____

135

2. A: Ápay a saanka a natúrog idi rabii?

   B: _____

3. A: Naggapuan ni Lélongmo?

   B: _____

4. A: Ania nga óras idi simmangpet da Mánongmo?

   B: _____

5. A: Ania ti ginátangmo?

   B: _____

6. A: Ania ti ar-aramídem?

   B: _____

7. A: Ania ti kinnanyo idiay balay da Teresita?

   B: _____

C. 1. Divide into groups.

   2. Your teacher will distribute a strip of paper to each of you. A sentence is typed on each of these strips. When the sentences are put together in the correct sequence, they will make a coherent narrative.

   3. You are given one minute to memorize the sentence on your strip of paper, then the teacher will collect the papers and throw them away.

   4. You have seven minutes to discover the correct sequence for your sentences and to be ready to say the story.

XI. WRITING PRACTICE

Write a detailed summary of the dialog.

XII. LISTENING PRACTICE

The following sentences are based on the dialog. Listen carefully as the teacher reads them to you. If you think the sentence is correct, say *Husto,* if it is not, say *Saan a husto,* and justify your answer.

136

A. Makaturtúrog ni A.
B. Parbángon idi simmangpet ti uliteg ni Burcio.
C. Naggapo idiay Tsína ti uliteg ni Burcio.
D. Alas dóse iti rabii idi simmangpet ti uliteg ni Burcio.
E. Sangapúlo a balot ti kinnan ni A.
F. Mangmangan ni A ti balot.
G. Mangmangan ni B ti balot.
H. Kayat únay ni A ti balot.
I. Kayat únay ni B ti balot.

Lesson Ten

I.   DIALOG: Playing Hooky

Study the following dialog. Try to understand the meaning of each sentence by referring to the literal translations in the box.

1

1. A: Kumusta ti klásem ita?

2. B: Nasayáat met, 'Tang.

2

3. A: Ania ti inarámidyo idiay eskuéla ita?

4. B: Nagbásakami, sa nag-súratkami, sa napan-kami idiay laybrari, sa nangankami idiay kapiteria.
. . . Ado ti inarámidmi. Iso met la nga iso ti ubrámi káda aldaw.

3

5. A: Sinno ti kaduam?

6. B: Dagiti kaeskueláak.

7. A: Napananyo?

8. B: Idiay eskuéla, 'Tang.

4

9. A: Ibagam ti pudno!

10. B: Awan ti napanak! Saludsúdenyo kenni Esteban.

11. A: Ápay ngarod a nagkol-ap ti prinsipalyo ditoy? Salsaludsúdennaka.

klásem	class-your
ita	now, today
nasayáat	fine
'Tang	Dad
nagbásakami	read-we
sa	then (sequence)
nagsúratkami	wrote-we
napankami	went-we
nangankami	ate-we
kapiteria	cafeteria
iso	it
met	also
la	only
ubrámi	work-our
káda	every
aldaw	day
kaduam	companion-your
napananyo	place-went-you
ibagam	tell-you
pudno	truth
awan	none
napanak	place-went-I
saludsúdenyo	inquire-you
kenni	from
nagkol-ap	called-up
prinsipalyo	principal-your
ditoy	here
salsalud-súdennaka	inquiring-he-you

138

II.   TRANSLATING THE DIALOG

Write a free translation of the dialog (i.e., a translation in natural English). Do it in pencil, and then check it against the translation in Appendix One. Make whatever corrections are necessary.

A:_____

B:_____

A:_____

B:_____

_____

A:_____

B:_____

A:_____

B:_____

A:_____

B:_____

A:_____

III.   LEARNING THE DIALOG

After the presentation of the dialog, two of you volunteer to write the dialog on the blackboard. One will write A's lines and the other B's lines. The rest of the class will close their books and dictate the dialog to the writers. Next, divide into pairs, one partner will face the blackboard and say A's lines. With his back to the blackboard, the others will say B's lines. A may prompt B if necessary. Change places.

IV.   ROLE-PLAYING

How would you say the dialog in the situations below?

A. A is acting nonchalant; B is acting over-excited.

B. A is serious; B is nervous.

C. A is concerned and worried; B is defiant.

V. VOCABULARY

Familiarize yourself with the following words you will need to use
in the following sections. Ask your teacher to help you pronounce
them correctly.

A. Nouns

babái	female, girl, woman
buok	hair
empleyádo	employee
galiéra	cockpit
laláki	male, man
manok	chicken
padaya	party
rúot	grass
tiangge, tiendáan	market
swapmit	swapmeet

B. Verbs

1. AG- (past tense NAG-)

nagballog	played hooky
nagláko	sold
naglúgan	rode

2. -UM- (past tense -IM- or -IMM-)

gimmátang	bought

3. -EN (past tense -IN-)

binisíta	visited
binúya	watched
kinartib	cut (with scissors)
kiníta	went to see, looked at
pinarti	killed (for food)
pinúted	cut off

sinagaysay	combed
sinaludsod	inquired
sinápol	searched for

4. -AN (past tense -IN—AN)

inayaban	called
kinol-ápan	called (on the telephone)
sinurátan	wrote to
tinulúngan	helped
binugkáwan	yelled at

5. I- (past tense IN- or IM-)

| impúlong | reported |
| insúrat | wrote |

VI.   CHANGING THE DIALOG

A. Using the situations below, and referring to the vocabulary section that you have just studied, how would you change:

PART 1 of the dialog?

1. B tells A that
$\begin{cases} \text{his classes were very good that day.} \\ \text{he didn't like his classes that day.} \\ \text{they did a lot of work in class.} \\ \text{they had a party in class.} \end{cases}$

2. A asks B how his
$\begin{cases} \text{teacher was that day.} \\ \text{friends were.} \\ \text{work was that day.} \\ \text{meeting was the night before.} \\ \text{lunch at the cafeteria was that noon.} \end{cases}$

PART 2 of the dialog?

1. A wants to know what B and his friends did
$\begin{cases} \text{at the party.} \\ \text{at the meeting.} \\ \text{at the market.} \\ \text{at the church.} \\ \text{at the swapmeet.} \\ \text{at the cockfight.} \\ \text{at their neighbor's house.} \\ \text{on their field trip.} \end{cases}$

141

2. A wants to know what B and his friends

- watched on television.
- ate at the restaurant.
- sang in the program.
- searched for in the grass.
- bought in the shopping center.
- did in their history class.
- did at home.
- did in the office.
- did with the chicken.
- did with their hair.

PART 3 of the dialog?

1. B says his companion was

- his brother.
- his girlfriend.
- his Ilokano teacher.
- his female classmate.
- his big dog.
- his doctor friend.

2. B says his companions were

- Ponso and his friends.
- his neighbors.
- his friends.
- his brothers and sisters.
- his father and mother.
- his teachers.

3. A wants to know who B

- visited.
- watched.
- went to see.
- asked.
- called (on the telephone).
- wrote to.
- called.
- helped.
- yelled at.

PART 4 of the dialog?

1. B says he didn't

- do anything.
- say anything.
- report anything.
- write anything.

2. B suggested asking
{
his teacher.
their principal.
Roman, his friend.
his classmate.
his co-worker.
his officemate.
}

3. It was B's
{
classmate
roommate
co-worker
officemate
boss
employee
co-teacher
lawyer
doctor
nurse
secretary
housemate
}
who called asking for him.

B. How would you change the dialog in the situations below?

1. B didn't like school that day. They did more activities than he had recounted.

2. Instead of the principal calling, B's teacher came by to inquire about B's absence.

3. B's mother went looking for him because she also received a phone call from the school.

VII. QUESTION AND ANSWER

With a partner, practice asking and answering these questions. Try asking other questions, too. Ask your teacher to give you the Ilokano for words you do not know. Speak only in Ilokano.

1. Kumusta kano ti kläse ni B iti daydiay nga aldaw?

2. Ania kano ti inar-arámid da B idiay eskuéla iti daydiay nga aldaw?

3. Sinno kano ti kadua ni B iti daydiay nga aldaw?

4. Napanan kano da B?

5. Sinno kano ti nagkol-ap idiay balay da B?

6. Sinno kano ti salsaludsúden ti prinsipal?

7. Ápay a kasla mabuteng ni B?

8. Ápay a kasla makaunget ti Tátang ni B?

VIII.   NOTES

A. Grammar

1. I- Verbs. Verbs which have an *i-* prefix are patient-focus verbs also, just like *-en* and *-an* verbs. The subject of the sentence is the patient. Most verbs that take *i-* are those in which the patient is moved (usually away from or with the actor) by the action of the verb:

a. Ibellengmo ti danom.
   Throw out the water.

b. Ipanmo daytoy páyong idiay uneg.
   Take this umbrella inside.

c. Ipaw-itko dagitoy bangbanglo idiay Pilipínas.
   I will send these perfumes to the Philippines.

d. Ikúyogmo ni Juan.
   Take Juan along.

Verbs of speech, such as *baga* (say), *arasáas* (whisper), and *pukkaw* (shout), are prefixes with *i-* when the subject is what is said. It can be considered a transmitted patient:

e. Ibagam ti pudno.
   Tell the truth.

f. Iyarasáasnanto kenka ti náganna.
   He will whisper his name to you.

2. Location. In Lesson Five, we introduced the locative determiner *iti*. A location need not be a place name, such as *Baguio,* or a common noun such as *balay* (house), a location is used as the locative determiner before a personal noun. It is translated as to, from, with, at, depending upon the meaning of the verb:

a. Ibagam kenni Marciano ti kayatmo.
   Tell (to) Marciano what you want.

144

b. Saludsúdenyo kenni Esteban.
   Ask (about it from) Esteban.

c. Mapanka kenni Rogelio.
   Go to Rogelio.

d. Kumúyogka kenni Rogelio.
   Go with Rogelio.

Iti and *kenni* are used before singular nouns. If the nouns are plural, the determiners are *kadagiti* and *kada:*

e. Itedmo dayta kankanen kadagiti ubbing.
   Give the rice cake to the children.

f. Agteléponoka kada Julian.
   Call up Julian's (Julian and his companions') place.

3. Auxiliary *sa* (then). Verbs which occur in sequence (i.e., where one action follows immediately after another action) often have the auxiliary *sa* before them. Since *sa* is an auxiliary, it does not have a linker between it and the verb. Also, because it is an auxiliary, pronouns are attached to it, rather than to the verb:

a. Nangankami, sákami nagbúya ti síne.
   We ate, then we watched a movie.

b. Nagdígosak, sáak natúrog.
   I took a bath, then I went to sleep.

4. *Iso met la nga isu.* This is an idiom, which translates as It is always the same or It is one and the same. It is based on a construction which has two identical root words joined by a linker and which means repeatedly or always:

sángit a sángit	always crying
túrog a túrog	always sleeping
lagto a lagto	always jumping

In Lesson Eight we noticed that when the pronoun *-mo* is attached to the negative auxiliary *di,* it does not reduce to *-m,* as we might expect, since it follows a vowel. Likewise, when *-mo* is attached to *sa* it does not reduce to *-m.* The full form *sámo* occurs, not *sam:*

c. Kiwárem dayta ágas sámo inumen.
   Stir the medicine, then drink it.

IX. EXERCISES

A. Study the following sentences in preparation for the exercises that will follow.

1. Mangibellengka ti basúra.
   Throw away some garbage.

   Ibellengmo ti basúra.
   Throw away the gar-
   bage.

2. Mangipanka ti pláka idiay uneg.
   Take some records inside.

   Ipanmo daytoy pláka
   idiay uneg.
   Take this record inside.

3. Mangikúyogka ti ubing.
   Take a child along.

   Ikúyogmo ta ubing.
   Take that child along.

4. Mangipaw-ítak ti kuarta.
   I'll send some money.

   Ipaw-itko ti kuarta.
   I'll send the money.

5. Mangisagánaka ti mainom.
   I'll prepare a drink.

   Isagának ti mainom.
   I'll prepare the drink.

6. Mangitúgotkayo ti kanen.
   Bring some food with you.

   Itúgotyo ti kanen.
   Bring the food with you.

7. Mangisublíta ti masétas.
   Let's return some plants.

   Isublíta ti masétas.
   Let's return the plants.

8. Mangibagáka ti burburtia.
   Tell a riddle.

   Ibagam diay burbur-
   tiam.
   Tell that riddle of yours.

9. Mangípalawagka ti maysa a
   pammáti.
   Explain a belief.

   Ipalawagmo ti
   pammátim.
   Explain your
   belief.
   Explain the belief
   of yours.

B. Write the correct form of the verb and the pronoun in the blank spaces of the following sentences. Choose from the verbs below.

kúyog	to go along, to take along	ited	to give
pukkaw	to yell	ákar	to transfer
subli	to return	kábil	to put

146

baga	to tell, to say	palawag	to explain
túgot	to bring	arasáas	to whisper
pan	to go, to take to	áwat	to pass

1. Itedmo_____man daytoy libro kenni Carlos?

Would you please give this book to Carlos?

2. _____daytoy singsingko idiay uneg ti kuarto.

I will take my ring into the room.

3. _____ti básona iti lamisáan.

She will put her glass on the table.

4. _____man ti leksion, Maestra?

Would you please explain the lesson, teacher?

5. _____ti náganmo kenkuana.

Whisper your name to him.

6. _____dayta libro idiay laybrari.

Return that book to the library.

7. Saan_____nga_____ti gayyemmo.

Do not take your friend along.

8. Dí_____kayat nga_____ ti náganna.

He does not want to call his name out.

9. _____ti nómerom.

Tell your number.

10. Ania a kanen ti kayat_____ nga_____?

What kind of food do they want to bring?

11. _____man dayta asin?

Would you please pass the salt?

12. Mangipankami ti sábong idiay balayyo.

We will take some flowers to your house.

13. Saan_____a_____ti
serbésa dita aysbaks.

Don't put any beer
in the refrigerator.

14. _____man ti papel?

Would you please give
me a paper?

15. _____ti kanen idiay
padaya.

Let us (all) bring
some food to the
party.

16. _____ti kaduána.

She will bring along a
companion.

17. _____man ti mangga.

Would you please pass
a mango?

C. Study the examples and write the appropriate determiners in the following sentences.

1. Itedko daytoy sábong iti ubing.

2. Ipaw-itna daytoy sapátos kenni Trining.

3. Ipanyo man dagitoy masétas kada Táta Pulon (Tata Pulon and his family).

4. Iyáwatmo man dagita lápis kadagiti estudiante?

5. Isublíta daytoy páyong_____Lucas.

6. lpukkawmo ti sungbatmo_____tattáo.

7. lpaw-itko dagitoy_____pamiliam.

8. Itedda ti lamisáanda_____Misis Cristobal (Mrs. Cristobal and her family).

D. Translate the sentences in C above.

1._____

2._____

3._____

4._____

148

5._____

6._____

7._____

8._____

E. Complete these sentences with a *sa* phrase.

1. Idi rabii, nangankami,   Last night, we ate;
                                              then we watched TV.

   _____

2. Iti rabii, uminom ti   At night, my child
   anakko ti gátas,   drinks milk; then he
                                              goes to sleep.

   _____

3. Káda bigat, agsipilió-ak,   Every morning, I
                                              brush my teeth; then I
                                              wash my face.

   _____

4. Káda rabii, agkararagkayo,   Every night, all of you
                                              pray; then leave.

   _____

5. Daítem dayta bádom,   Sew your dress; then
                                              wash it.

   _____

6. Lutuem dayta nateng,   Cook the vegetable;
                                              then put it on a plate.

   _____

7. Iwáek ti karne,   I slice the meat; then I
                                              cook it.

   _____

X.   COMMUNICATION ACTIVITY

A. Select the things that you did yesterday from the following list.
   Write them down and the teacher will then ask you to read
   them to the class. You may add things you did that are not on
   the list. Discuss your activities with the class.

   Gimmátangak ti pangaldaw.   I bought lunch.

   Bimmúlodak ti lápis.   I borrowed a pencil.

149

Immútangak ti kuarta.	I borrowed some money.
Immáyak ditoy kláse.	I came (here) to class.
Naglúganak iti bus.	I rode a bus.
Naglúganak iti karro.	I rode in a car.
Nagnáak.	I walked.
Nagdígosak.	I took a bath.
Nagdiram-ósak.	I washed my face.
Nagsipilió-ak.	I brushed my teeth.
Naginanáak.	I rested.
Nagádalak.	I studied.
Nagbásaak.	I read.
Nagsúratak.	I wrote.
Nagtrabáho-ak.	I worked.
Nagmeriendáak.	I had a snack.
Nangaldáwak.	I ate lunch.
Namigátak.	I ate breakfast.
Nangrabií-ak	I ate dinner.
Napának idiay kapiteria.	I went to the cafeteria.
Napának idiay bangko.	I went to the bank.
Napának idiay tiendáan.	I went to the store.
Natúrogak.	I slept.

B. One of you volunteer to tell the class in Ilokano what you did between the time you left for school and this class period. Half of the class will listen, the other half will write down what you say. Two of the listeners will then try to recall everything that you have done in the correct sequence. The writers will check the accuracy of their statements from their notes.

C. Study the following words in preparation for the activity that follows.

ikábil	to put
ipan	to take to
ited	to give
ibelleng	to throw away
isubli	to return

150

ingáto	to raise
ibaba	to lower
idúlin	to put away
iruar	to take outside
iserrek	to bring inside
ilemmeng	to hide
idisso	to put down
ipisok	to put into

1. Collect a set of transferable objects such as pen, paper, stone, comb, trash, etc. and write an Ilokano description of it on an index card:

   nalabbága a sagaysay

   ababa a lápis

2. Place the objects on a table, and give the index cards to the teacher.

3. Form two rows and face each other. The teacher will give one index card each to the even-numbered members of Team 1 and one each to the odd-numbered members of Team 2.

4. Then the card holders take turns giving instructions to the person opposite them on the other team. Instructions must include the verb to get (using either *mangála* or *aláen* correctly) and must contain a verb from the list above, telling the opponent what to do with the item listed on the index card, e.g.,

   a. Mangálaka ti bato ta ibellengmo.
       Get a stone and throw it away.

   b. Aláem ti nalabbága a sagaysay ta itedmo kenni John.
       Get the red comb and give it to John.

5. If either the question or the response is improperly given the person remains standing.

6. The team with the largest number of sitting members after every card holder has given his instruction is the winner.

D. 1. Divide into groups of three.

    2. Write a continuation of the dialog in seven minutes.

151

3. Practice the dialog, including what you have written, for five minutes.

4. Say the dialog with a partner without using your notes. The third member of your group will act as your prompter.

XI.   WRITING PRACTICE

A. Write a narrative of not less than fifteen sentences about what you did in school and at home last Monday. Use actor-focus verbs *(ag-, mang-, -um-,* and *ma-)* and patient-focus verbs *(-en, -an* and *i-).* Use the appropriate tense where necessary.

XII.   LISTENING PRACTICE

Listen to the story as the teacher reads it to you twice.

"Dagiti Agtatákaw"

Nagsardeng ti karro iti sanguánan ti balay. Bimmaba ti tallo a lal-láki. Napanda iti likudan ti balay. Binúongda ti táwa a sarming iti maysa a siled. Kalpasanna, immúlida iti táwa.

Innálada dagiti aláhas ken kuarta nga adda iti aparador. Innálada met ti telebision ken sabali pay nga al-alikámen iti úneg ti balay. Kalpasanna naglúganda iti karróda ket pimmánawda.

Idi simmangpet ti pamilia nga aggígian idiay balay, nangayabda ti pulis. Immay ti dua a pulis ket sinaludsodda no ania ti napa-sámak.

A.   The words below are arranged in the sequence of the story. Tell the story using the words as a guide.

nagsardeng	stopped
bimmaba	came down
napan	went
binúong	broke
immúli	went up
innála	took
innála	took
naglúgan	rode

pimmánaw	left
simmangpet	arrived
nangayab	called
immay	came
sinaludsod	inquired

B. Your teacher will give you a copy of the narrative with the verbs missing. Supply the correct verbs without referring to the book.

C. Retell the story in Ilokano.

D. Answer the questions based on the story.

1. Ania ti nagsardeng iti sanguánan ti balay?

_____

_____

2. Sinno ti rimmuar iti karro?

_____

_____

3. Sadinno ti napanan dagiti tallo a lalláki?

_____

_____

4. Ania ti inarámidda iti táwa?

_____

_____

5. Kalpasan a binúongda ti sarming, ania ti inarámidda?

_____

_____

6. Ania dagiti innálada?

_____

_____

7. Kalpasan nga innálada ti aláhas, telebision ken daddúma pay, ania ti inarámidda?

_____

_____

8. Ania ti inarámid ti pamilia idi simmangpetda idiay balay?

_____

_____

9. Mano ti immay a pulis?

_____

_____

10. Ania ti sinaludsod dagiti pulis?

_____

_____

11. Ania ti napasámak?

_____

_____

154

Lesson Eleven

I. DIALOG: Doing Homework

Study the following dialog. Try to understand the meaning of each sentence by referring to the literal translations in the box.

1

1. A: Nalpasmo ti 'homework' mon?

2. B: Saan pay, 'Tang.

2

3. A: Isardengmo dayta ta inka agádal. Patayem dayta tíbi.

4. B: Mabiit láeng, 'Tang. Nganngáni malpásen.

5. A: Patayem dayta tíbi, kunak ket!

3

6. B: Mabiit láeng. Masápol a buyáek daytoy ta . . .

7. A: Leppasem pay ti trabáhom, sákanto agbúya ti tíbi.

4

8. B: 'Tang, masápol a buyáek daytoy.

9. A: Ápay, ania dayta buybuyáem, aya?

nalpasmo	finished-you
isardengmo	stop-you
inka	go-you
agádal	study
patayem	kill-you
dayta	that (near)
tíbi	TV
mabiit	shortly
láeng	only
nganngáni	nearly
malpásen	will be finished-already
kunak	say-I
ket	(emphasis)
masápol	necessary
buyáek	watch-I
daytoy	this
leppasem	finish-you
pay	first
trabáhom	work-your
sákanto	then-you-future
ápay	why
ania	what
buybuyáem	watching-you
aya	anyway

II. TRANSLATING THE DIALOG

Write a free translation of the dialog (i.e., a translation in natural English). Write in pencil, and then check it against the translation in Appendix One. Make whatever corrections are necessary.

155

A:_____

B:_____

A:_____

B:_____

A:_____

B:_____

A:_____

B:_____

A:_____

III.   LEARNING THE DIALOG

After the presentation of the dialog, divide into groups of two. You and your partner will build the dialog from memory, and write it on index cards—A's lines on one card and B's lines on another. Read it to your teacher for corrections. Afterwards, say the dialog to each other, with the person who has the A card saying B's lines, and the person with the B card saying A's lines. Both partners will check each other from memory or with the help of the cards, if necessary.

IV.   ROLE-PLAYING

How would you say the dialog in the situations below?

A.   A (a parent) is reading the paper and notices B (a child) in front of the TV. B continues to watch TV and is very engrossed in it. B ignores an order from A.

Variations

1.   A is at the top of the stairs; B is in the living room.

2.   A is authoritative; B is showing annoyance at the interference.

156

V. VOCABULARY

Familiarize yourself with the following words that you will need to use in the following sections. Ask your teacher to help you pronounce them correctly.

A. Nouns

bádo	dress
dalikan	stove
kómiks	comic book
istírio	stereo
prográma	program
rádio	radio
sílaw	light

Gerunds

panagádal	studying
panagbása	reading
panagdáit	sewing
panagdalos	cleaning
panaginnaw	dishwashing
panaglúto	cooking
panagmakinília	typing
pannangan	eating
panagsúrat	writing
panagurnos	tidying up

B. Verbs

1. AG-

agbása	to read
agdalos	to clean up
agdengngeg	to listen
agdígos	to take a bath, or a swim
aginnaw	to wash dishes
aglaba	to do laundry

157

agmakinília   to type

agsúrat   to write

2. -EN

denggen   to listen

VI.   CHANGING THE DIALOG

A. Using the situations below, and referring to the vocabulary section that you have just studied, how would you change:

PART 1 of the dialog?

1. B hasn't finished her {
work.
assignment.
dress.
studying.
reading.
sewing.
cleaning.
dishwashing.
cooking.
typing.
eating.
writing.
tidying up.

PART 2 of the dialog?

1. A wants B to stop what she is doing so that she can go {
to work.
type.
do the laundry.
cook.
eat.
read.
write to his aunt.
clean up.

PART 3 of the dialog?

1. A wants B to {
turn off the radio.
turn off the tape recorder.
turn off the light.
turn off the stove.
turn off the stereo.

158

PART 4 of the dialog?

1. B says she has to
$$\begin{cases} \text{listen.} \\ \text{watch.} \\ \text{read.} \\ \text{cook.} \\ \text{write.} \\ \text{do (it.)} \\ \text{finish (it.)} \end{cases}$$

B. How would you change the dialog in the situations below?

1. A wants B to stop watching TV in order to wash the dishes.

2. B is listening to the radio.

3. B is reading a comic book.

4. A wants B to turn the TV on to another channel because he wants to watch a certain program, but B insists that what is on is her homework for history class.

5. A wants B to go to bed, even though she is still doing her homework.

VII. QUESTION AND ANSWER

Practice asking and answering these questions with a partner. Try asking other questions. Ask your teacher to give you the Ilokano for words you do not know. Speak only in Ilokano.

1. Nalpas ni B ti 'homework'nan?

2. Ania ti kayat ni A nga aramíden ni B?

3. Ania ti kayat ni A a patayen ni B?

4. Ania kano ti nganngáni malpásen?

5. Ania ti masápol a buyáen ni B?

6. Ania ti kayat ni A a leppasen ni B sakbay nga agbúya ti tíbi?

7. Apay ngata a masápol a buyáen ni B ti prográma iti tíbi?

8. Ania ngata ti buybuyáen ni B?

159

VIII. NOTES

A. Grammar

1. Deliberate versus Involuntary. Ilokano patient-focus verbs, i.e., those that have an *i-, -en,* or *-an* affix, may be either deliberate or involuntary. When they occur without the prefix *ma-* (or *na-* if past tense), they are deliberate. The action is done on purpose. If the action just happened to be done without deliberate intention, or is involuntary, *ma-* also occurs as a prefix on the verb. Notice the way *-en* does not appear when *ma-* is used.

Deliberate	Involuntary
i-	mai-
-an	ma—an
-en	ma-

The past tense of the involuntary form of a verb uses *na-,* rather than *ma-:*

   a. Ay, nagastok ti kuartam!
       Oh, I spent your money by mistake!

   b. Nakítam ni Rosita itattay?
       Did you happen to see Rosita before?

Sometimes *ma-* (past tense *na-*) is used to give the meaning of ability:

   c. Naibellengmo diay danom?
       Were you able to throw out the water?

   d. Nadalusak daydiay balay.
       I was able to clean the house.

   e. Nabagkatna ti maléta.
       He was able to pick up the suitcase.

2. Notice that words with double consonants in the middle, lose the first vowel and the first of the middle consonants when *ma-* or *na-* is attached to it:

leppas	nalpas	finished
bussog	nabsog	satisfied
punno	napno	filled

160

kesset	nakset	burnt
bettak	nabtak	cracked
seddáaw	nasdáaw	surprised
kelláat	nakláat	startled

3. Conjunction *ta* because, so. This conjunction has two basic meanings: purpose and reason. Context usually enables us to know which of the two meanings it has. In sentence a it can only mean purpose, and can be translated as and or so. In sentence b it can only mean reason, and it is translated as because.

  a. Isardengmo dayta ta inka agádal.
     Stop that and go study.

  b. Matúrogak ta nabannógak.
     I'm going to sleep because I'm tired.

4. *Kuna* say. The verb *kuna* is an irregular patient-focus verb. It does not have any affix unless it is explicitly past tense or completed. If the verb precedes the quotation, the verb and the quotation are joined by a linker:

  a. Kunána nga dína kayat ti mangan.
     He says that he doesn't want to eat.

  b. Kinunána nga nalpasna ti trabáhonan.
     He said that he had finished his work.

IX.   EXERCISES

  A. Change the following deliberate verbs to involuntary verbs. Remember that -*en* does not appear in the involuntary verbs.

  1. ibelleng   <u>naibelleng</u>   thrown out by mistake

  2. idúlin   _____   put away by mistake

  3. isubli   _____   returned by mistake

  4. ibaga   _____   told by mistake

  5. ikábil   _____   put by mistake

161

6. dungpáren   <u>nadungpar</u>   hit accidentally

7. kitáen   _____   happened to see

8. basáen   _____   happened to read

9. ikkaten   _____   happened to be removed

10. pigísen   _____   tore accidentally

11. labaan   <u>nalabaan</u>   got washed

12. baddekan   _____   got stepped on

13. tupráan   _____   got spat on

14. mantsáan   _____   got stained

15. rugitan   _____   got soiled

B. Translate the following sentences.

1. I will read your letter.   _____

2. I happened to read the news.   _____

3. I'm going to throw out this

    garbage.   _____

4. I threw out your medicine by

    mistake.   _____

5. I will tell your secret.   _____

6. I told your secret by

    mistake.   _____

7. Remove your glasses.   _____

8. He happened to take off his   _____

   glasses.   _____

9. Norma will wash the   _____

   stockings.   _____

10. Norma washed the stockings   _____

    by mistake.   _____

11. Don't get your pants dirty.   _____

12. My pants got dirty.   _____

C. Translate the following sentences, keeping in mind the difference between the two meanings of *ta*. Refer to the Grammar Notes.

   1. Mangálaka ti sábong ta   _____

      itedmo kenni Rose.   _____

   2. Iddepem dayta tíbi ta inka   _____

      matúrogen.   _____

   3. Mangának ta mabisínak.   _____

   4. Agpáyongka ta agtudtúdo.   _____

   5. Nagáwid ni Benny ta   _____

      masakit.   _____

   6. Agsapátosta ta inta agbúya   _____

      ti síne.   _____

163

7. Uminomka ti ágas ta

   nakapsotka. _____

8. Agsardengkan ta inka _____

   aginanan. _____

9. Aginanákan ta _____

   nabannogkan. _____

10. Umayka ta manganka. _____

D. Write the correct verbs in the blank spaces.

"_____-mo man daytoy,"
      throw away
kuna ni Elsa kenni Elmo.

"Please throw this away," Elsa said to Elmo.

"Saanmo nga_____ta
               throw away
masápolko," kuna ni Elmo.

"Don't throw it away, (because) I need it," Elmo said.

"_____-mo ngarod, ta
      put away
agdaldalósak ditoy," kuna ni Elsa.

"Put it away then, (because) I'm cleaning here," Elsa said.

"Saan, ta_____-k," kuna
            launder
ni Elmo.

"No, (because) I'll wash it," said Elmo.

"_____-mo ngarod dita
      put
paglabaan," kuna ni Elsa.

"Put it in the laundry, then," Elsa said.

"Ala wen," insungbat ni
Elmo. "Mánang Elsa,_____-m
                        see

ti anteóhosko ditoy? sinaludsod
ni Elmo.

"Okay," Elmo answered. "Manang Elsa, did you happen to see my glasses (here)?" Elmo asked.

"Saan,_____-m idiay
      look
kábinet," kuna ni Elsa.

"No, look in
the cabinet,"
Elsa said.

"Awan idiay," kuna ni Elmo.
"Amangan no_____-mo dita
      put
kuarto," kunana pay.

"They're not
there," Elmo said.
"You might have
put them in the
room," he added.

"Saan, inka sapúlen idiay
uneg. Amangan no_____-mo,"
      put away
kuna ni Elsa.

"No, go and
look inside. You
might have put
them away," Elsa
said.

"Saan a báli," kuna ni Elmo,
sa rimmuar.

"Never mind,"
Elmo said and then
went outside.

E. Below is a list of actions that people often do in sequence. Write the sequence marker and the appropriate pronoun in the blank spaces.

1. Agdígosak, sáak agbádo.

I take a bath, then I get dressed.

2. Labaak ti bádok, sáko ibalaybay.

I wash my clothes, then I hang them up.

3. Ngalngálek ti kanek,_____
tilmúnen.

I chew my food, then I swallow it.

4. Ukisak ti saba,_____kanen.

I peel the banana, then I eat it.

5. Asukáram ti kapem,_____
inumen.

Put sugar in your coffee, then drink it.

6. Kupinenna ti lúpotna,_____
idúlin.

He folds his clothes, then he puts them away.

7. Innáwanyo ti pinggan,_____
punásan.

Wash the dishes, then wipe them.

8. Surátenna,_____basáen.	She writes it, then she reads it.
9. Tumakdertayo,_____magna.	We stand up; then we walk.
10. Manganta,_____aginana.	We eat, then rest.

X.   COMMUNICATION ACTIVITY

    A. Divide into groups of three. Then make a list of things you have to do or finish this semester, such as errands, assignments, or projects. Take turns telling your group these things, making sure to use forms such as *masápol* (necessary), and *aramíden* (to do) or *leppasen* (to finish).

    B. Write a note reminding yourself of things to be done, and telling yourself when you will finish these things. Make a list of tasks you already have completed.

    C. Explain how to cook a simple recipe. Specify the procedure, using sequence markers between the sentences.

XI.   WRITING PRACTICE

    A. Assume that B's assignment was to watch a TV program and to write a report about it. Decide what B was watching and write a report for him in Ilokano.

166

Lesson Twelve

I. DIALOG: Looking for Something Lost

Study the following dialog. Try to understand the meaning of each sentence by referring to the literal translations in the box.

1

1. A: Ayan tay librok ditoy?

2. B: Kitáem dita rabaw ti lamisáan.

3. A: Awan met ditoy.

2

4. B: Sapúlem idiay siled ta basbasáem idiay idi rabii.

5. A: Awan idiay. Sinápolko idiáyen.

3

6. B: Baka adda dita sírok ti katre.

7. A: Awan dita. Sinápolko ditan.

4

8. B: Ay, inka kitáen dita abay ti tugaw ta kasla nakítak dita itay!

9. A: Ay, wen, gáyam!

ayan	where
tay	that (earlier)
librok	book-my
ditoy	here
kitáem	look-you
dita	there (near)
rabaw	top
lamisáan	table
awan	none
sapúlem	search-you
idiay	there
siled	room
basbasáem	reading-you
idi	past
rabii	night
sinápolko	searched-I
idiáyen	there (far)-already
baka	maybe
adda	there is
sírok	under
katre	bed
ditan	there (near)-already
ábay	side
tugaw	chair
kasla	as-though
nakítak	saw-I
itay	before
wen	yes
gáyam	surely

II. TRANSLATING THE DIALOG

Write a free translation of the dialog (i.e., a translation in natural English). Do it in pencil, and then check it against the translation in Appendix One. Make whatever corrections are necessary.

A:_____

B:_____

A:_____

B:_____

A:_____

B:_____

A:_____

B:_____

A:_____

III.   LEARNING THE DIALOG

After the presentation of the dialog, divide into two groups. Help each other learn the dialog for five minutes. Put away your notes. Each group will then assign one person to be its representative to write on the board. The writers are given five minutes to write the dialog on the board. The errors are then counted (a missing or misspelled word is considered to be an error). Whoever has the largest number of errors is the loser. Repeat the procedure with two more writers, or as necessary to complete the dialog.

IV.   ROLE-PLAYING

How would you say the dialog in the situations below?

A. A is hard of hearing.

B. A and B are both drunk.

C. A is frantic because she is late for class.

D. A is annoyed and suspects that B might have picked up the book and misplaced it.

V.   VOCABULARY

Familiarize yourself with the following words that you will need to use in the following sections. Ask your teacher to help you pronounce them correctly.

A. Nouns

antiparra, antióhos	eyeglasses
arítos	earrings
bestído/a	dress
blúsa	blouse
kuentas	necklace
medias	socks
padiáma	pajama
palda	skirt
pantalon	trousers
pulséras	bracelet
relo	watch
sagaysay	comb
sinílas	slippers
sinturon	belt
singsing	ring
diario, pagiwarnak	newspaper
dágom	sewing needle
gitára	guitar
kuarta	money
mágasin	magazine
makinília	typewriter
pláka	record
sipilio	toothbrush
sungka	a wooden game board
súrat	letter
tulbek	key
agdan	steps
aparador	cabinet
aysbaks	refrigerator
bánio	bathroom
baol	trunk, chest
bentána,	window

indáyon	hammock, swing
katre, káma	bed
kuarto	room
kusína	kitchen
labábo	sink
ladáwan	picture
lamisáan	table
masétas	ornamental plant
rídaw, puerta	door
sálas	living room
sopa	sofa
tugaw	chair

B. Adjectives

nabengbeng	thick
nadagsen	heavy
naingpis	thin
nalag-an	light

C. Locatives

ábay	beside
asideg	near
baet/nagbaetan	between
ígid	edge
kannigid	left
kannawan	right
likudan	behind
makinkan-nigid	left side
makinkan-nawan	right side
rabaw	on top of
sanguánan	in front of
sikigan	side

sírok	underneath
tengnga	middle
uneg	inside

VI. CHANGING THE DIALOG

A. Using the situations below, and referring to the vocabulary section that you have just studied, how would you change:

PART 1 of the dialog?

1. A is looking for her

{
shoes.
socks.
slippers.
blouse.
pants.
pajamas.
skirt.
dress.
belt.
comb.
toothbrush.
watch.
necklace.
ring.
earrings.
bracelet.
eyeglasses.
magazine.
newspaper.
key.
money.
guitar.
letter.
record.
}

2. B wants A to look
   for it
$$\begin{cases} \text{on the steps.} \\ \text{at the door.} \\ \text{in the living room.} \\ \text{in the kitchen.} \\ \text{in the bathroom.} \\ \text{near the cabinet.} \\ \text{under the bed.} \\ \text{next to the table.} \\ \text{in front of the TV.} \\ \text{behind the sofa.} \\ \text{between the chair and the} \\ \qquad \text{table.} \end{cases}$$

PART 2 of the dialog?

1. A was
$$\begin{cases} \text{sewing it.} \\ \text{cutting it up (with scissors).} \\ \text{cleaning it.} \\ \text{wiping it.} \\ \text{washing it.} \\ \text{making it the night before.} \\ \text{viewing it the day before.} \\ \text{typing it the week before.} \\ \text{using it that Sunday.} \end{cases}$$

PART 3 of the dialog?

1. B thinks it might be

{

in front of the bed.
behind the sofa.
behind the stove.
next to the swing.
near the chair.
next to the typewriter.
behind the ornamental plant.
under the ornamental plant.
behind the picture.
in front of the picture.
in front of the radio.
between the cabinet and the
    trunk.

PART 4 of the dialog?

1. B thinks he saw it

{

next to the table.
near the television.
on top of the radio.
under the table.
on top of the big book.
under the thick book.
in front of the cabinet.
in the middle of the small bed.
inside the bathroom.
to the left of the sink.
inside the refrigerator.

B. How would you change the dialog in the situations below?

1. A is looking for her pictures. B has never seen them but suggests places where A might find them.

2. A is looking for a sewing needle.

3. A is looking for her guitar that B was using the night before.

4. The locations are different.

5. A and B go with friends for a picnic. After unloading, they want to play *sungka,* but can't find it anywhere. They finally find it under the seat of the car.

6. The owner of the book is at the door waiting for the book; so A is very embarrassed and keeps apologizing to him. The owner, who is in a hurry, is trying very hard to be polite.

VII.   QUESTION AND ANSWER

Get a partner and practice asking and answering these questions with him or her. Try asking other questions, too. Ask your teacher to give you the Ilokano for words you do not know. Speak only in Ilokano.

1. Ania ti sapsapúlen ni A?

2. Adda kadi ti libro ni A iti rabaw ti lamisáan?

3. Ania kano ti ar-aramíden ni A iti napalábas a rabii?

4. Adda kadi idiay siled ti libro ni A?

5. Adda kadi ti libro ni A iti sírok ti katre?

6. Nakakitáan kano ni B iti libro ni A?

7. Ayan ti libro ni A?

8. Ápay ngata nga adda iti ábay ti tugaw ti libro ni A?

VIII.   NOTES

A.   Grammar

1. Locative Existentials—Definite

PREDICATE	LOCATION	SUBJECT
Existential word	Locative word or phrase	Definite noun phrase

adda	idiay tugaw	ti libro

In Ilokano you can assert or deny the existence of something, or say that something is or is not at some place, with the use of the words *adda* (there is) and *awan* (there is none).

When the subject is at the end of the sentence, it is definite, that is, it usually is translated with the:

    a. Adda idiay siled ti púsa.
        The cat is in the room.

    b. Awan idiay siled ti púsa.
        The cat is not in the room.

When one of the locative words, *ditoy, dita,* and *(d)idiay,* occur following *adda,* the two words combine as follows:

adda	plus	ditoy	becomes	addadtoy
adda	plus	dita	becomes	addadta
adda	plus	idiay	becomes	addaddiay

Another set of demonstrative existentials is used when drawing attention to some object, as when someone is looking for something and the speaker knows where it is. These existentials probably are combinations of *adda* and the *daytoy* demonstrative set:

    a. Addaytoy ti sapsapúlem.
        Here is what you are looking for.

    b. Addayta ti sapsapúlem.
        There (near) is what you are looking for.

    c. Addaydiay ti sapsapúlem.
        There (far) is what you are looking for.

2. Locative Existential—Indefinite

PREDICATE	SUBJECT	LOCATION
Existential word	Indefinite noun phrase	Locative word or phrase
adda	libro	idiay tugaw

175

An indefinite subject occurs between the existential word and the locative. An indefinite subject following *adda* does not have any determiner preceding it, as in example a:

Following *awan,* an indefinite subject can either have no determiner or the subject determiner *ti,* as in example b:

    a.   Adda púsa idiay siled.
         There is a cat in the room.

    b.   Awan púsa idiay siled.
         Awan ti púsa idiay siled.
         There isn't any cat in the room.

Notice that if a determiner is used with a subject following *adda* it becomes definite:

    c.   Adda ti púsa idiay siled.
         The cat is in the room.

3. Subject Determiners. The most general determiner used before subject common nouns is *ti*. However, there is another set of determiners that can be used before subject common nouns which parallel the demonstratives in meaning. In fact, they are short forms of the demonstratives. They are not true demonstratives, however, because they cannot occur on their own without a following noun, neither can a linker occur between the short demonstrative and the noun. Notice the meanings of the subjects in the following examples:

    a.   Aláem man toy bagko.
         Please get this bag of mine.

    b.   Nasakit ta úlom?
         Do you have a headache?

    c.   Kitáem diay billit.
         Look at the bird.

    d.   Ayan tay librok ditoy?
         Where is my book that was here before?

    e.   Tinawágan ni Margarita di bosmo.
         Margarita called up your former boss.

IX.   EXERCISES

A. Translate the following sentences.

1. Here it is.   _____

2. There it is. (near)   _____

3. There it is over there.   _____

4. There is your comb. (near)   _____

5. Here is your necklace.   _____

6. There are your earrings   _____

    over there. (far)   _____

7. It is there. (near)   _____

8. It is here.   _____

9. It is there. (far)   _____

10. My socks are out   _____

    there. (far)   _____

11. The newspaper is here.   _____

12. Her belt is there. (near)   _____

13. Your ring is here on top   _____

    of the table.   _____

14. Amanda's keys are inside   _____

    the room. (near)   _____

15. Mother's bracelet is

over there under the

car. (far)

    _____

    _____

    _____

B. What would you say if your friend

    1. was looking for her slipper and you tell her that it is where you are?

       Addadtoy ti sinílasmo.

    2. was looking for her key and you picked it up and handed it to her?

       Addaytoy ti tulbekmo.

    3. came to your house and handed you a record that she borrowed from you?

       _____

    4. pointed out the newspaper to you?

       _____

    5. pointed out your child who is on the other side of the street?

       _____

    6. was throwing out a box and you mentioned that her letter was inside it?

       _____

C. Study the notes on existential constructions and then do the exercises below. Take note of the difference in position of the definite and indefinite noun phrases. What would you say if:

    1. You don't own a dog but when you walked into your room, you saw one.

       _____

2. You were not expecting to see some *bási* in the kitchen and when you walked into the kitchen, you saw a jug of it.

_____

3. You happened to touch a mango under your pillow and you were surprised.

   Ni, _____!

4. You were surprised to see a car in the garage.

   Ni, _____!

5. You have been looking for your toothbrush and Ana says it is where she is.

   Adda ditoy ti sipiliom. _____

6. Belinda happens to find your blouse that you have been looking for behind the sofa.

_____

7. Vicky tells Letty that the key that she lost is on the floor beside the table.

_____

8. Maria was surprised to find their neighbor's newspaper near the cabinet, and inquires about it.

_____

X.   COMMUNICATION ACTIVITY

A. The teacher will label all of the objects in your classroom and the different parts of the classroom with index cards having both the Ilokano and English names on them. Familiarize yourself with the names. The class will then divide into four groups. When the teacher gives a command *(Agtaraykayo idiay táwa,* or *Agtakderkayo iti ábay ti pisarra),* one person from each group promptly executes the command. The first one to do so correctly earns a point for her group.

B. Tell the class what is in a) a classroom, b) a restaurant, c) a kitchen, d) an office, e) a market.

C. Tell the class what is found

in an office that is not in a market.
in a bedroom that is not in a living room.
in a restaurant that is not in a classroom.
in a park that is not in a library.

D. Get a picture of your family or friends. Describe the positions of the individuals in relation to one another.

E. You are lost, so you call your friend and ask him to come and get you. Explain to him where you are located in relation to various landmarks.

F. Call your sister and ask her to bring an object to school that you left at home. Explain to her exactly where you think you left it. Your sister will try to locate it while you are on the phone.

G. Help your partner to build a part of your neighborhood using rods or blocks. He will follow your instruction as to the position of the buildings in relation to one another.

XI. WRITING PRACTICE

You are talking to a friend who is planning to visit your hometown. Describe your hometown in detail and tell her what it has and what it lacks. Use positive and negative existentials, i.e., *awan* and *adda*.

Lesson Thirteen

I. DIALOG: Changing Residence

Study the following dialog. Try to understand the meaning of each sentence by referring to the literal translations in the box.

1

1. A: Ápay nga umákarkayo manen?

2. B: Nakatagtagari ngamin idiay lugarmi.

2

3. A: Ápay a natagari idiay?

4. B: Asideg ngamin iti pageskueláan. Nagringgor dagiti ubbing. Sa asideg pay iti pagparadáan.

3

5. A: Natagtagari pay idiay pagakáranyo, a, ta asideg iti 'freeway'.

6. B: Saan a báli ta adda erkondisionna. No irikepmo dagiti táwa, sámo luktan ti erkondísion, saanmo a mangngeg ti tagari iti ruáren.

7. A: Ay sus, nagastar únay iti koriénte!

ápay	why
umákarkayo	move-you
manen	again
nakatagtagari	very-noisy
ngamin	reason adverb
lugarmi	place-our
natagari	noisy
asideg	near
pageskueláan	school
nagringgor	very-noisy
ubbing	children
sa	also
pay	moreover
pagparadáan	parking lot
natagtagari	noisier
pagakáranyo	place-move to-your
saan	not
báli	worth
erkondísionna	air-conditioner-its
no	if
irikepmo	close-you
táwa	window
sámo	then-you
luktan	open
saanmon	not-you-anymore
mangngeg	hear
tagari	noise
ruar	outside
sus	short for Jesus
nagastar	costly
koriénte	electricity

181

II.   TRANSLATING THE DIALOG

Write a free translation of the dialog (i.e., a translation in natural English). Do it in pencil, and then check it against the translation in Appendix One. Make whatever corrections are necessary.

A:_____

B:_____

A:_____

B:_____

_____

A:_____

_____

B:_____

_____

A:_____

III.   LEARNING THE DIALOG

After the presentation of the dialog, divide into three groups. One member from each group gives a sentence for the teacher to write on the board. Continue taking turns until the dialog is completed.

IV.   ROLE-PLAYING

How would you say the dialog in the situations below?

A.   B, A's father, doesn't want A to move so far away, so he is discouraging B from shifting. B is resisting his father's meddling.

B.   A is hard of hearing.

C.   A and B are on the phone. They have a poor connection.

V.   VOCABULARY

Familiarize yourself with the following words which you will need to use in the following sections. Ask your teacher to help you pronounce them correctly.

A. Nouns

ábang	rent
al-alia	ghost
bartikéro	drunkard
estéro	drainage canal
kabbalay	housemate
tiendáan	market, store
pabrika	factory
pagbasuráan	garbage dump
plása	plaza, market
pulis	police
sílaw	light
sementerio	cemetery

B. Verbs

1. AG-

agap-ápa	quarreling
agbusína	to sound a horn

2. MANG-

mangayab	to call

3. MA- (stative past tense NA-)

natay	died

4. -UM-

pumánaw	to leave

5. MAKA- (abilitative)

makangngeg	able to hear

6. MA- (accidental, past tense NA-)

nakíta	saw

C. Adjectives

naángot, nabangsit	smelly
nangáto	high
nangína	expensive
natrápik	heavy traffic
túleng	deaf

comparative

ad-ado	more
naang-ángot	more smelly
napudpúdot	hotter
nataptápok	dustier
natraptrápik	heavier traffic

intensive

nakabutbuteng	very scary
nakadugdugyot	very filthy
nakaluklúko	very troublesome
nakapudpúdot	very hot
nakarugrugit	very dirty

D. Adverb

agmalmalem	all day

E. Sentence Modifier

sigúro	maybe

VI. CHANGING THE DIALOG

A. Using the situations below, and referring to the vocabulary section that you have just studied, how would you change:

PART 1 of the dialog?

1. A is wondering why B and his companions are
   {
   leaving
   calling the police
   going out
   quarreling
   } again.

184

2. B says that $\left\{\begin{array}{l}\text{their place is very dirty.}\\\text{their place is very hot.}\\\text{their house is very small.}\\\text{their housemates are very filthy.}\\\text{their neighbors are trouble-}\\\text{makers.}\end{array}\right.$

PART 2 of the dialog?

1. A wants to know why $\left\{\begin{array}{l}\text{the traffic is heavy.}\\\text{it's smelly.}\\\text{there are a lot of people.}\\\text{there are a lot of ghosts.}\\\text{it's scary.}\end{array}\right.$

PART 3 of the dialog?

1. A says that it $\left\{\begin{array}{l}\text{is hotter.}\\\text{is dustier.}\\\text{is more smelly.}\\\text{has heavier traffic.}\end{array}\right.$

2. B says $\left\{\begin{array}{l}\text{they are not home during the day,}\\\text{he can't hear because he is deaf,}\\\text{they don't toot their horns,}\end{array}\right\}$ anyway

B. How would you change the dialog in the situations below?

1. A is moving because the garbage dump near their house is very smelly. But B points out that the place they are moving to is worse because it is near a fish factory. A doesn't care about that.

2. A is moving because it is very noisy living near the airport. B points out that the rent of the place he is moving to is exorbitant. Moreover, it is crowded.

3. A is moving because he says he has heard ghosts in the house. He even claims he has seen them. He thinks it is because someone died in the house. B points out that there will probably be more ghosts in the place he is moving to because it is near a cemetery.

VII. QUESTION AND ANSWER

Get a partner and practice asking and answering these questions with him or her. Try asking other questions, too. Ask your teacher to give you the Ilokano for words you do not know. Speak only in Ilokano.

1. Ania ti salsalúdsuden ni A kenni B?
2. Ápay nga umákar kano da B?
3. Ápay a natagari kano idiay lugar da B?
4. Ápay a natagtagari kano idiay pagakáran da B?
5. Ania kano ti aramíden da B, tapno saanda a mangngeg ti tagari iti ruar?
6. Ket sika, kayatmo kadi ti balay nga adda erkondísionna? Ápay?
7. Kayatmo kadi ti aggian iti asideg ti 'freeway'? Ápay (saan)?

VIII.   NOTES

A. Grammar

1. Comparative Adjectives. In English, when we compare the same quality in two different objects, we either use the word more, e.g., more beautiful, more successful, or we add a suffix -er to the adjective, e.g., happier, sweeter. In Ilokano, we add a CVC- reduplicative prefix. This prefix comes between the *na-* prefix (if there is one), and the root word:

napintas	pretty	napinpintas	prettier
dakkel	big	dakdakkel	bigger

Remember that if the root does not begin with a consonant only the first VC- is reduplicated:

ababa	short	ab-ababa	shorter
asideg	near	as-asideg	nearer

If there is no middle consonant in the root, only the first CV́- is reduplicated, but the vowel is made long:

nalaing	smart	nalálaing	smarter
naguápo	handsome	nagúguápo	more hand-some

2. Plurals Of Nouns. We mentioned earlier (Lesson Three) that *ti áso* could mean the dog or the dogs, but that *dagiti áso* could only mean the dogs. Notice that in these examples, the word for dog did not change whether it was singular or plural. It is possible, however, to make a plural form of common nouns like *aso,* by adding a CVC- prefix. The different forms of CVC- are the same as were discussed earlier for comparative adjectives, i.e., VC- if the word starts with a vowel, and CV- if there is no middle consonant:

kaykáyo	trees
tugtugaw	chairs
as-áso	dogs
al-alíngo	wild pigs
wáwáig	streams

There is a set of nouns referring to human beings that require the plural form to be used if they are in fact plural. These nouns have a different way of forming the plural. They double the consonant that follows the first vowel of the word. Some also require the reduplication of the first CV- of the word. Compare the plural words in the following list.

	singular	plural
grandchild	apóko	appóko
father	ama	amma
mother	ina	inna
child	ubing	ubbing
offspring	anak	annak
young man	baro	babbaro
young woman	balásang	babbalásang
old man	lakay	lallakay
old woman	baket	babbaket
male	laláki	lalláki
female	babái	babbái
spouse	asáwa	assáwa
person	táo	tattáo

3. Reason Sentence. A reason sentence frequently is used as a response to an *ápay* (why) question. The word *ngamin* (that's why) is placed after the first main word of the reason sentence:

Question: Ápay a nagsakitka?
How come you got sick?

Answer: Nagsakítak ta natuduának ngamin.
I got sick because I got rained on.

4. Idiom: *saan a báli.* This phrase, which literally means "It is of no value," is used in situations where in English, we would normally say "Never mind," or "It doesn't matter."

5. *dengngeg* listen, hear. This verb has several forms which require changes in the root. When the meaning listen is meant, this verb can be used in either actor-focus (if the patient is indefinite), or patient-focus (if the patient is definite). Either *ag-* or *-um-* actor-focus affixes can be used. Since *dengngeg* has a double *ng* in the middle of the word, when *-um-* is used, the rule described in Lesson Eight operates, the first vowel and one of the doubled consonants is dropped:

Actor-focus

Agdengngegta iti radio — Let's listen to the radio.
Dina kayat ti dumngeg. — He does not want to listen.

When the patient-focus affix *-en* is used, the final vowel and one of the double consonants are dropped, *dengngegen* becomes *denggen:*

Patient-focus

Denggenyo ti ibagak kadakayo.
Listen to what I say to you.

In Lesson Eleven we mentioned that the prefix *ma-* gives either an involuntary, or ability meaning to the verb. The verb hear is the involuntary equivalent of listen, so *ma-* plus *dengngeg* is used to mean hear, or can hear. Notice that this forms an irregular verb, *ma-dengngeg* becomes *mangngeg.*

Denggem ti kampána.
Listen to the bell.

Mangngegko ti kampána.
I can hear the bell.

IX.   EXERCISES

A. Learning the Forms

Below is a list of adjectives. Based on the examples given, write the comparative forms in the right-hand column. If you have any difficulty, ask your teacher to help you.

ADJECTIVES	COMPARATIVE	TRANSLATION
nabaknang	nabakbaknang	richer
nakuttong		
nalagda		
napuskol		
nakapsot		
napardas		
nasayáat		
namaga		
nabasa		
napúdot		
natáyag		
natápok		
nangína		
nalaka		

189

nabanglo		
nabangsit		
nasingpet		
natangken		
naános	naan-ános	more kind, more patient
naímas		
nainávad		
naingpis		
naulímek		
naalas		
naasok		
naalsem		
naapgad		
nadungngo		
naunget		
nalaing	nalálaing	smarter, better
naláad		
naguápo		
atiddog	at-atiddog	taller
ababa		

akíkid   _____   _____

akába   _____   _____

asideg   _____   _____

adayo   _____   _____

ado   _____   _____

ulbod   _____   _____

baro   barbaro   newer

bassit   _____   _____

madi   _____   _____

dáan   _____   _____

báak   _____   _____

B. Question and Answer

    1. Sinno ti napinpintas, ni   1._____

       Marilyn Monroe wenno ni   _____

       Ingrid Bergman?   _____

    2. Sinno ti nagúguápo, ni Elvis 2._____

       Presley wenno ni Robert   _____

       Redford?   _____

    3. Sinno ti nabakbaknang, ni   3._____

       Rockefeller wenno ni Ted   _____

       Kennedy?   _____

4. Ania ti nanginngína, ti   4._____

    Datsun wenno ti Porsche?   _____

5. Ania ti dakdakkel, ti Luzon   5._____

    wenno ti Mindanao?   _____

6. Ania ti nalaklaka, ti karro   6._____

    wenno ti sapátos?   _____

7. Ania ti naim-ímas, ti adóbo   7._____

    wenno ti dinengdeng?   _____

8. Ania ti nabangbanglo, ti   8._____

    kalatsutsi wenno ti kamia?   _____

9. Ania a lugar ti maymayat, ti   9._____

    Hawaii wenno ti Chicago?   _____

10. Ania a karne ti natang-   10._____

    tangken, karne ti báboy   _____

    wenno karne ti manok?   _____

C. Write the plural forms of the nouns in the following sentences:

1. Nagála dagiti ubbing   The children
   ti_____.   gathered flowers.
      sábong

2. Ginátangko dagitoy a_____.   I bought these
                báso   glasses.

3. Inlákona dagiti_____.   She sold the
          lamisáan   tables.

4. Napúkaw dagiti_____   His visitors'
            sapátos   shoes were lost.
   dagiti bisítana.

5. Pinerdi dagiti nalóko nga estudiante dagiti_____ relo idiay eskuéla.

The troublesome students destroyed the clocks in the school.

6. Inayabanna dagiti_____ áso dagiti kaarrúbana.

He called his neighbor's dogs.

7. Inabel ni Ando dagiti _____nga ilaklákona. ules

Ando wove the blankets that he is selling.

8. Kinalbo ti lakay dagiti _____dagiti annakna úlo ta nakapudpúdot.

The old man shaved his childrens' heads because it was very hot.

9. Imbelleng ti babái ti nagado a_____. buok

The woman threw away so much hair.

10. Napankami kadagiti_____ wáig a nalitnaw (ti danomna).

We went to the streams with clear water.

D. Read and study the following narrative in preparation for the exercises that follow it.

'Ti Pamiliámi'

'Our Family'

Nagado ti annak ni Tátangko. Sangapúlo ket limákami. Wen, ado ti kakabsatko-walo ti babbái, ken innem ti lalláki. Sangapúlon ti appóna.

My father has so many children. There are fifteen of us. Yes, I have many brothers and sisters—eight sisters and six brothers. My father already has ten grandchildren.

Káda Paskua, ado ti tattáo idiay balay ta umay ámin dagiti kakaba-gian ni Tátangko. Umay bumisíta amin dagiti sangapúlo ket dua a kakabsatna ken dagiti kakaanakan ken appókoda. Umay met dagiti

Every Christmas, there are many people at the house, because all my father's rela-tives come over. His twelve brothers and

193

kakasinsin, ik-íkit ken ul-ulitegna. Adon kadakuáda ti babbaket ken lallakay, ngem napipigsáda pay láeng. Napipigsáda kano ta kanáyon a mangmanganda ti salúyot ken buggúong.

Iti rabii, agkakanta ken aggigitára dagiti kakabagiak a babbaro ken babbalásang. Natagari únay ta aggaáyam met dagiti ubbing.

Kanáyon a nagrambak ti Paskuámi!

sisters, and all of their nieces, nephews, and grandchildren come to visit. His cousins, aunts, and uncles also come. Many of them are old men and women, but they are all still strong. They are strong they say because they always eat *salúyot* (a green, leafy vegetable, that is slimy when cooked) and *bagoong* (a salted, fermented fish used for seasoning).

In the evening, the young men and women who are my relatives sing and play guitar. It's very noisy because the children also play around.

Our Christmases are always so festive!

1. Write the plural words that occur in the narrative. Write their singular forms and indicate whether they are nouns, verbs, or adjectives. Classify them as best you can.

   a. appóko   apóko   noun

   b. _____   _____   _____

   c. _____   _____   _____

   d. _____   _____   _____

   e. _____   _____   _____

f. _____ _____ _____

g. _____ _____ _____

h. _____ _____ _____

i. _____ _____ _____

j. _____ _____ _____

k. _____ _____ _____

l. _____ _____ _____

m. _____ _____ _____

n. _____ _____ _____

o. _____ _____ _____

p. _____ _____ _____

q. _____ _____ _____

r. _____ _____ _____

s. _____ _____ _____

2. Answer the questions based on the narrative. Use complete sentences.

   a. Mano ti annak ni Tátangko? <u>Sangapúlo ket lima ti annak ni Tátangmo.</u>

   b. Mano ti kakabsatko? _____

   c. Mano ti kakabsatko a babbái? _____

d. Mano ti kakabsatko a

   lalláki?

e. Mano ti appo ni Tátangkon? _____

   _____

f. Sinno ti umay bumisbisíta _____

   kadakami káda Paskua? _____

g. Mano ti kakabsat ni _____

   Tátangko? _____

h. Sinno dagiti kakabagian ni _____

   Tátangko nga bumisbisíta _____

   kadakami káda Paskua? _____

i. Sinno dagiti napipigsa pay _____

   láeng? _____

j. Apay kano a napipigsáda _____

   pay láeng? _____

k. Ania ti ar-aramíden dagiti _____

   kakabagiak a babbaro ken _____

   babbalásang no rabii? _____

l. Ápay a natagari dagiti _____

   ubbing? _____

X.   COMMUNICATION ACTIVITY

A.   1. The class will divide into pairs. One of each pair will turn so that he cannot see the blackboard; his partner will face the blackboard.

2. The teacher will place a series of different colored cards on the board, each marked with a price, the lowest price to the left, the highest to the right.

3. The students who cannot see the blackboard will be given sets of colored cards, the same as those on the board, but not marked with prices.

4. The goal is to arrange the cards in the same order as those on the board by asking one's partner in Ilokano whether a given color is more expensive than another, or whether a given color is cheaper than another. The partner may only respond with *'Wen'* or *'Saan'*.

B.   You have just taken a world tour. Your roommate is planning a world tour next year. She asks you to compare the different places you have been to so she can plan how much time she should spend in each place.

C.   You and your partner are teachers. You are comparing your students.

D.   You and your partner are students. You are comparing your teachers.

XI.   WRITING PRACTICE

Each student will think of a sentence containing a comparative adjective and write it on the board until a coherent dialog is created. For example:

A: Daytoy ti gatángem ta nalúluom.

B: Diak kayat. Nalúluom dayta ngem basbassit.

C: Basbassit daytoy ngem nasamsam-it.

D: Nasamsam-it ngem nanginngína.

(ken daddúma pay)
(etc.)

LISTENING PRACTICE

Your teacher will read the following sentences. If you think the statement is true, tell her so. If you think it is not true, tell her why it is not. Write the translations in the right hand column. Ask your teacher for words you do not know.

A. 1. Nabaknang ni Jackie   1._____

       Onassis.   _____

    2. Nalagda ti Volkswagen.   2._____

    3. Napardas ti Porsche.   3._____

    4. Nakuttong ni Twiggy.   4._____

    5. Nalaing ti bosko.   5._____

    6. Naímas ti pinakbet.   6._____

    7. Naalsem ti mangga.   7._____

    8. Naguápo ni Paul   8._____

       Newman.   _____

    9. Bassit ti Oahu.   9._____

    10. Asideg ti California.   10._____

B. 1. Nabakbaknang ni   1._____

       Rockefeller ngem ni   _____

       Jackie Onassis.   _____

    2. Nalaglagda ti Volks-   2._____

       wagen ngem ti Datsun.   _____

198

3. Naparpardas ti Porsche   3._____

   ngem ti Toyota.   _____

4. Nakutkuttong ni Twiggy   4._____

   ngem ni Raquel Welch.   _____

5. Nalálaing ti bosko ngem   5._____

   ti bosmo.   _____

6. Naim-ímas ti pinakbet   6._____

   ngem ti dinengdeng.   _____

7. Naal-alsem ti pias ngem   7._____

   ti naáta a manga.   _____

8. Nagúguápo ni Robert   8._____

   Redford ngem ni Paul   _____

   Newman.   _____

9. Basbassit ti Oahu ngem   9._____

   ti Luzon.   _____

10. As-asideg ti California   10._____

    ngem ti Guam.   _____

C. Your teacher will read to you sentences substituting English adjectives in place of the Ilokano form. Supply the appropriate neutral or comparative form depending upon the context.

Lesson Fourteen

I.   DIALOG: Planning a Trip

Study the following dialog. Try to understand the meaning of each sentence by referring to the literal translations in the box.

1

1. A: Ania ti kapintá-san a lugar idiay Pilipínas?

2. B: Ápay, agbaka-sionka?

3. A: Wen.

2

4. B: Kaano ti panag-bakasionmo?

5. A: Intuno Disiem-bre, ta mayat ti tiempo.

3

6. B: Ado ti napipin-tas a lugar idiay, ngem diak ammo no ania ti kapintásan.

7. A: Saan a báli. Kumúyogakto láengen iti 'tour'.

4

8. B: Kaano ti ipapan ti 'tour'?

9. A: Intuno kínse ti Disiémbre'

10. B: Ay, mabayag pay gáyam!

kapintásan	most-beautiful
lugar	place
kaano	when
panag-bakasionmo	time-vacation-your
intuno	(future)
Disiembre	December
ta	because
mayat	fine
tiempo	weather
ado	many
napipintas	beautiful (plural)
ngem	but
diak	not-I
ammo	know
no	if
ania	what
saan	not
báli	worth
kumúyogakto	go with-I-future
láengen	just-already
ipapan	time-go
kinse	fifteen
mabayag	long time
pay	yet, still
gáyam	so, really

II.   TRANSLATING THE DIALOG

Write a free translation of the dialog (i.e., a translation in natural English). Do it in pencil, and then check it against the translation in Appendix One. Make whatever corrections are necessary.

A:_____

B:_____

A:_____

B:_____

A:_____

B:_____

_____

A:_____

B:_____

A:_____

B:_____

III.   LEARNING THE DIALOG

After the presentation of the dialog, help your teacher memorize it. Do not let up until she has it word-perfect.

IV.   ROLE-PLAYING

How would you say the dialog in the situations below?

A. A and B are hurriedly eating their lunch.

B. A's spouse is nearby and she doesn't want him to know about her plans to go to the Philippines yet. B is not aware of the situation.

C. A is very excited because his father just gave him some money to take a trip to the Philippines

V. VOCABULARY

Familiarize yourself with the following words that you will need to use in the following sections. Ask your teacher to help you pronounce them correctly.

A. Nouns

bario	barrio, village
íli	town
kabbalay	housemate
maléta	suitcase
pasdek	building
pléte	fare
probinsia	province
restawran	restaurant
siudad	city

B. Time Gerunds

ipapánaw	leaving time
isasangpet	arriving time
isusubli, panagsubli	returning time
iyaákar, panagákar	shifting time
iyaális, panagális	shifting time
iyuumay	coming time
panagbiáhe	travelling time
panagbisíta	visiting time
panageksámen	examining time
panaggátang	buying time
panagláko	selling time
panangiláko	time to sell (it)

C. Superlative Adjectives

kadaánan	oldest
kalagdaan	most durable

202

kalakaan	cheapest
kangatuan	tallest
kangináan	costliest
kapardásan	fastest
kaasitgan	nearest
kasayaátan	best

D. Months

Enéro	January
Pebréro	February
Márso	March
Abril	April
Máyo	May
Húnio	June
Húlio	July
Agósto	August
Septiémbre	September
Octubre	October
Nobiémbre	November
Disiémbre	December

E. Play Vocabulary Sweepstakes. (See Lesson Two.)

VI. CHANGING THE DIALOG

A. Using the situations below, and referring to the vocabulary section that you have just studied, how would you change:

PART 1 of the dialog?

1. A wants to know what the
{
best car is.
best movie in town is.
fastest car is.
nearest restaurant is in the city.
oldest building is.
cheapest radio is at the Appliance House.
most expensive restaurant is in Honolulu.
}

203

PART 2 of the dialog?

1. B wants to know when A $\begin{cases} \text{is taking his exam.} \\ \text{and his companions will} \\ \quad \text{have a party.} \\ \text{is taking his trip.} \\ \text{is visiting his relatives.} \\ \text{is going back to work.} \end{cases}$

PART 3 of the dialog?

1. B says that there
   are many $\begin{cases} \text{nice cars.} \\ \text{expensive television sets.} \\ \text{cheap radios.} \\ \text{delicious kinds of food.} \end{cases}$

PART 4 of the dialog?

1. B wants to
   know when
   A's $\begin{cases} \text{friends} \\ \text{father} \\ \text{brother} \\ \text{older sister} \\ \text{boss} \\ \text{classmate} \\ \text{fellow-worker} \\ \text{housemate} \\ \text{relative} \\ \text{neighbor} \\ \text{lawyer} \end{cases}$ is/are $\begin{cases} \text{going to take} \\ \quad \text{the exam.} \\ \text{going to take} \\ \quad \text{a vacation.} \\ \text{traveling.} \\ \text{visiting.} \\ \text{coming.} \\ \text{leaving.} \\ \text{going.} \\ \text{returning.} \\ \text{moving.} \end{cases}$

2. B wants to know when A $\begin{cases} \text{is going home.} \\ \text{is returning.} \\ \text{going to Maui.} \\ \text{arriving.} \\ \text{is leaving.} \\ \text{going on vacation.} \\ \text{taking his exam.} \\ \text{selling his bike.} \\ \text{buying a car.} \\ \text{moving to his new house.} \end{cases}$

3. A says she is leaving on $\begin{cases} \text{December 1.} \\ \text{January 31.} \\ \text{February 22.} \\ \text{March 15.} \\ \text{April 4.} \\ \text{May 27.} \\ \text{June 2.} \\ \text{July 4.} \\ \text{August 16.} \\ \text{September 9.} \\ \text{October 30.} \\ \text{November 26.} \end{cases}$

B. How would you change the dialog in the situations below?

1. B is A's boss.

2. A wants to know what the cheapest new car is at Honolulu Motors. He is in a hurry to buy a car because his girlfriend is arriving.

3. A wants to know what the most durable suitcase is because he wants to buy one in May for his trip to the Philippines in January.

4. A is going to study Ilokano in the summer. She will go with the Philippine Study Tour to the Ilocos.

5. A wants to know what the cheapest fare is to the Philippines so that he can visit his relatives.

VII. QUESTION AND ANSWER

Get a partner and practice asking and answering these questions with him or her. Try asking other questions, too. Ask your teacher to give you the Ilokano for words you do not know. Speak only in Ilokano.

1. Ania ti salsaludsúden ni A kenni B?

2. Anianto ti aramíden ni A?

3. Kaanonto ti panagbakasion ni A?

4. Ápay a Disiémbre ti kayat ni A a panagbakasion?

5. Ammo kadi ni B no ania ti kapintásan a lugar idiay Pilipínas?

6. Anianto ti aramíden ni A idiay Pilipínas tapno makítana dagiti napipintas a lugar idiay?

7. Kaanonto ti ipapan ni A idiay Pilipinas?

8. Asidég kadin a pumánaw ni A?

VIII.   NOTES

A. Grammar

1. Superlative Adjectives.

| ka- | Adjective | -an |

To form a superlative adjective, Ilokano uses the affix combination *ka—an*, e.g.,

karinggúran	noisiest
kalam-ekan	coldest
kaasitgan	closest
kapudáwan	fairest

2. Plural of Adjectives. In English, we usually only form plurals with nouns. Ilokano, however, sometimes uses a plural adjective when the following noun is plural:

Nasalun-at dagita nalulukmeg nga ubbing.
Those plump children are healthy.

To form the plural of an adjective a reduplication prefix is used. This prefix is called CV-, standing for the first consonant and first vowel of the root. Compare the singular and plural forms of the following adjectives.

singular	plural
nalukmeg	nalulukmeg
naringgor	nariringgor
napintas	napipintas

If a root word starts with a vowel, like *ababa* (short) there is usually no reduplication even if the noun is plural. It is not usual to say *Aababa dagiti lapisda* (Their pencils are short).

206

3. Time Gerunds. Recall that in Ilokano, when asking a *sadinno* (where) question, the verb which occurs in the subject is made into a locative gerund with the affix combination *pag—an:*

    a. Sadinno ti pagbakbakasiónam?
       where do you take your vacation?

When the question word is *kaano* (when), the verb which occurs in the Subject is made into a time gerund, *Kaano ti panagbakasionmo?* (When is your vacation-time?)

There are several different ways to form a time gerund, depending upon the kind of verb that forms the base of the gerund. The following table shows the main verb affixes and their corresponding time gerund affixes.

Verb	Time Gerund
ag-	panag-
mang-	panang-
ma-	iCV-
-um-	iCV-

The affix iCV- means a combination of i- and a reduplicative prefix which consists of the first consonant and vowel of the root, as described in Section Two of these notes.

    b. (agbakasion   to take a vacation)
       Kaano ti panagbakasionmo?
       When will you take a vacation?

    c. (mangála   to get)
       Kaano ti panangálam iti sueldom?
       When will you get your salary?

    d. (mapan   to go)
       Kaano ti ipapanmo?
       When will you go?

    e. (pumánaw   to leave)
       Kaano ti ipapánawmo?
       When will you leave?

Notice that verbs such as *ákar* (transfer) which can take either *-um-* or *ag-*, use either *iCV-*, or *panag-* to form the time gerund.

If the root begins with a vowel, only the vowel is reduplicated and *y* is inserted before the first vowel, e.g., *iyaákar, iyuúli,* etc.

The verb *umay* (come) has a regular time gerund *iyaay,* and an irregular form *iyuumay,* which treats *umay* as a root.

IX.   EXERCISES

A. Practicing the Forms

Based on the examples given below, write the superlative forms of the adjectives in the right-hand column. If you have any difficulty, ask your teacher to help you.

ADJECTIVE	SUPERLATIVE	TRANSLATION
nabaknang	kabaknángan	richest
nakuttong		
nalagda		
napuskol		
nakapsot		
napardas		
nasayáat		
namaga		
nabasa		
napúdot		
natáyag		

natápok _____ _____

nangína _____ _____

nalaka _____ _____

nabanglo _____ _____

nabangsit _____ _____

nasingpet _____ _____

natangken _____ _____

naános _____ _____

naímas _____ _____

naináyad _____ _____

naingpis _____ _____

naulímek _____ _____

naalas _____ _____

naasok _____ _____

naalsem _____ _____

naapgad _____ _____

naunget _____ _____

nalaing _____ _____

naláad _____ _____

naguápo _____ _____

atiddog _____ _____

ababa

akíkid

akába

asideg

adayo

ado

ulbod

baro

bassit

madi

dáan

báak

B. Question and Answer

1. Sinno ti kapintásan nga   1._____

   artista idiay Hollywood?   _____

2. Ania ti kaimásan a lúto   2._____

   ti Pilipíno?   _____

3. Sinno ti kapigsáan a   3._____

   táo iti ámin a lúbong?   _____

4. Ania ti kadakkelan nga   4._____

   estádo ti Amérika?   _____

5. Sinno ti kabaknangan   5._____

   a babái iti ámin a lúbong?   _____

6. Sadinno ti kalam-ekan a   6._____

   lugar ditoy lúbong?   _____

7. Sinno ti kalaingan nga   7._____

   artista iti ámin a lúbong?   _____

8. Ania ti kabassitan nga   8._____

   estádo ditoy Amérika?   _____

9. Ania ti kaatiddugan a   9._____

   karayan ditoy América?   _____

10. Ania ti kangatuan a bantay 10._____

    iti ámin a lúbong?   _____

X. COMMUNICATION ACTIVITY

DOMINGGO	LÚNES	MARTES	MIERKOLES	HUÉBES	BIERNES	SÁBADO
8:00 Napan idiay simbáan 9:00 Nagáwid	6:00 Nagriing 6:30 Naglúto ti pamigatna 7:00 Namigat 7:30 Napan nagtrabáho idiay Restawran Gánas 8:00 Nangrugi ti trabáhona	5:45 Nagriing ↑	↑	↑	↑	9:00 Nagriing 10:00 Namigat 11:00 Napan idiay Ala Moana Beach aginggánat' 1:30
12:00 Nangaldaw 1:00 Naginana	10:00 Nagmerienda 12:00–1:00 Nangaldaw	→	→	12:00 Nangaldawda kenni Pilar idiay Sampagíta Cafe 1:00 Intulodna ni Pilar	↑	1:30 Nagáwid 2:10 Nagdígos

2:00–3:00 Nagbásaiti diario 3:15 Nagmerienda 3:40 Napan idiay tiendáan	3:00–3:15 Nagbreyk, nagmerienda	3:00–3:15 Nagsiáping iti breykna	3:00–3:15 Natúrog iti breykna	3:15 Nagsubli iti trabáhona	4:00 Nagáwid 5:00 Nagrubuat 5:30 Dinagasna ni Pilar	2:00 Nangaldaw 4:00 Nagténis idiay Diamond
6:00 Naglúto ti pangrabii 7:00 Nangrabii 8:00 Naginnaw 8:30 Nagbúya ti tíbi 11:30 Natúrog	6:00 Simmangpet iti balayna 6:30 Naglúto ti pangrabiina 7:00 Nangrabii 8:00 Nagbúya ti tíbi 11:45 Natúrog	8:00 Nagténis 9:00 Nagdígos 9:30 Nagbása 12:15 Natúrog	8:00 Nagbisíta kenni Pilar a nobiána	8:00 Nagay-áyam ti solitario 10:00 Natúrog	6:30 Napan iti padaya 1:00 Nagáwid 2:00 Natúrog	6:00 Nagáwid 6:30 Nagdígos 7:00 Nangan 8:00 Nagbúya ti síne 10:30 Nagáwid 11:00 Nagdígos 11:30 Natúrog

Tata Lauro's Schedule

213

A. Review Tata Lauro's schedule for last week. Answer the following questions in complete sentences based on the information in that schedule.

1. Kaano ti ipapan ni Táta Lauro idiay simbáan?

   Idi Dominggo ti ipapanna.

2. Ania nga óras ti panamigatna idi Lúnes?

   Alas siéte ti panamigatna.

3. Ania nga óras ti panangaldawna?

   Alas dóse ti panangaldawna.

4. Ania nga óras ti panagriingna idi Sábado?

   Alas nuébe ti panagriingna idi Sábado.

5. Kaano ti panagbisítana kenni Pilar?

   Idi rabii ti Mierkoles ti panagbisítana kenni Pilar.

6. Kaano ti pannanganda kenni Pilar idiay Sampagíta Cafe?

   Idi Huebes ken Biernes ti pannanganda kenni Pilar idiay Sampagita Cafe

7. Ania nga óras ti panangrugi ti trabáhona?

8. Ania nga óras ti ileleppas ti trabáhona?

9. Ania nga óras ti panaglútona ti pangrabiína?

10. Ania nga óras ti panaginnawna?

11. Sinno ti binisítana idi alas otso ti Mierkoles?

214

12. Sinno ti kadua ni Táta Lauro

    a nangaldaw idi alas dóse ti

    Huebes idiay

    Sampagita Cafe?   _____

13. Ania ti inarámidna idi   _____

    alas kuartro ti Sábado?   _____

14. Sadinno ti nagtenísan ni   _____

    Táta Lauro idi Sábado?   _____

15. Ania nga óras ti pannatúrogna?   _____

                                  _____

16. Sadinno ti pagtrabtrabahuan   _____

    ni Táta Lauro?   _____

B. Using the *Guinness Book of World Records,* make a list of sentences in which some person, place, or thing is described by an adjective in the superlative degree. Divide into teams, and using your notes, ask the opposing team to supply the correct answers to twenty questions such as *Sinno ti kapigsáan a tao iti lúbong?* (Who is the strongest man in the world?)

C. Find a partner and ask each other questions based on the information on Tata Lauro's schedule. Ask your teacher for words you do not know. (Arrows on the chart indicate the same schedule as the previous day.)

XI.   WRITING PRACTICE

A. Make a schedule of your own activities for the coming week. Exchange it with your partner. Write a report about your partner's schedule.

215

B. Each student will write a sentence containing a superlative adjective on the board until a coherent dialog is created. For example:

A: Daydiay ti kaababaan nga eksámentayo.

B: Wen, ngem daydiay ti karigátan.

C: Saan, daydiay ti kalakaan nga eksámentayo.

(ken daddúma pay)

XII. LISTENING PRACTICE

A. Listen and Repeat

Your teacher will read the following sentences. Listen carefully to them and say *wen* or *saan*. Give your opinion if you say *saan*. Afterwards, write the translations in the right-hand column.

1. Ti Vatican ti kabassitan

    1._____

    a pagilian ditoy lúbong.

    _____

2. Ti Honda ti kalakaan a

    2._____

    karro ditoy Hawaii:

    _____

3. Ti Mindanao ti kadakkelan

    3._____

    a púro idiay Pilipínas.

    _____

4. Ti Sears Roebuck idiay

    4._____

    Chicago ti kangatuan a

    _____

    pasdek ditoy lúbong.

    _____

5. Ni Lawrence Olivier ti

    5._____

    kalaingan nga artista idiay

    _____

    Hollywood.

    _____

6. Ni Robert Redford ti   6._____

   katarakian nga artista a   _____

   laláki.   _____

7. Ni Ingrid Bergman ti   7._____

   kapintásan nga artista a   _____

   babái.   _____

8. Ti Unibersidad ti Hawaii ti   8._____

   kadakkelan nga unibersidad   _____

   ditoy Hawaii.   _____

9. Ti Concorde ti kapardásan   9._____

   nga eropláno ditoy lúbong.   _____

10. Ti Mayon ti kapintásan a   10._____

    bulkáno idiay Pilipinas.   _____

B. Listen carefully as your teacher reads the following story to you twice. Listen for words that are not familiar to you and write them down. Ask your teacher for their meanings.

"Ii Padayámi"

Idi lawásna, nagdaya ti klásemi iti Ilokano. Daydiay ti karambákan a padayámi ita a tawen. Nagtokar da Mila ken Lisa ti piano ken nagkantáda pay. Nalálaing nga agtokar ni Mila, ngem napinpintas ti tímek ni Lisa. Naggitára met ni Rosa.

Ado ti naímas a kanen idiay padaya. Dua a kita ti pinakbet ti intúgot ni Efren. Maysa nga adda karnéna ken maysa nga awan karnéna. Naim-ímas daydiay adda karnéna ta kayatko ti karne ti báboy.

Nagletsonkami met ti báboy. Pinílimi ti kabassitan a báboy idiay "Waialua Piggery" ta isu ti kalakaan.
Nagsasálakami aginggánat' alas dos ti parbángon. Nagáwidkami iti alas tres.

C. Answer the following questions about the story you have just heard.

1. Kaano ti panagdaya ti kláse ti Ilokano?

_____

_____

2. Ania ti inarámid da Mila ken Lisa?

_____

_____

3. Ania met ti inarámid ni Rosa?

_____

_____

4. Sinno ti nalálaing nga agtokar ti piáno, ni Mila wenno ni Lisa?

_____

_____

5. Sinno ti napinpintas ti tímekna, ni Mila wenno ni Lisa?

_____

_____

6. Ania ti ado idiay padaya?

_____

_____

218

7. Mano a kíta ti pinakbet ti intúgot ni fren?

8. Ápay a naim-ímas kano daydiay maysa a kíta ti pinakbet?

9. Ania pay ti inarámid dagiti estudiante idiay padaya?

10. Ápay a daydiay kabassitan a báboy ti pinílida idiay "Waialua Piggery"?

11. Ania ti inarámidda aginggánat' alas dos?

12. Ania nga óras idi nagáwidda?

D. Divide into two groups. While the teacher reads the narrative to you again, check to see how the words in the following list are used. When she has finished, a person from Group One will give one of the words to a person from Group Two. This person must create a sentence using the word which is consistent with the narrative, and then must choose a word for someone in Group One to use in a sentence. Points are scored for correct sentences.

idi láwasna

padaya

nagtokar

nagkanta

nalálaing

napinpintas

naggitára

ado

kíta

adda karnéna

awan karnéna

naim-ímas

báboy

nagletson

kabassitan

kalakaan

aginggána

nagáwid

E. Retell the story in English.

F. Retell the story in Ilokano.

Lesson Fifteen

I.   DIALOG: Borrowing Money

Study the following dialog. Try to understand the meaning of each sentence by referring to the literal translations in the box.

1

1. A: Adda kuartam?

2. B: Mano ti masá-polmo?

3. A: Sangapúlo a do-liar koma.

2

4. B: Ay, awan ti san-gapúlo a doliarko. Ápay a masápolmo ti kuarta, aya?

5. A: Adda ngamin deytko.

3

6. B: Ápay, díka pay nagsueldo, aya?

7. A: Saan man, ngem gimmátangak ti baro a sapátos ken pantalonko idi kalman. Naibúsen ti sueldok.

4

8. B: Dumáwatka kada Tátangmo.

9. A: Wen, koma, ngem awan met da Tátangko.

adda	there is
kuartam	money-your
mano	how much
masápolmo	need-you
sangapúlo	ten
doliar	dollar
koma	wish, hope
awan	there is none
kuarta	money
ápay	why
deytko	date-my
ngamin	reason adverb
pay	yet
nagsueldo	paid
saan man	on the contrary
ngem	but
gimmátangak	bought-I
baro	new
sapátos	shoes
pantalonko	pants-my
idi	remote past marker
idi kalman	yesterday
naibúsen	used up-already
sueldok	pay-my
dumáwatka	ask-you
Tátangmo	father-your
ayanda	place-their
addáda	there-they
agbakbakasionda	vacationing-they
sáyang	too bad
ngarod	then
aramídem	do-you

221

10. B: Ápay, ayanda?

11. A: Addáda idiay
Ilocos.
Agbakbaka-
sionda.

12. B: Ay, sáyang! Ania
ngarod ti
aramidem?

II.   TRANSLATING THE DIALOG

Write a free translation of the dialog (i.e., a translation in natural English). Do it in pencil, and then check it against the translation in Appendix One. Make whatever corrections are necessary.

A:_____

B:_____

A:_____

B:_____

_____

A:_____

B:_____

A:_____

_____

B:_____

A:_____

B:_____

A:_____

B:_____

III.   LEARNING THE DIALOG

After the presentation, divide into two groups. Group One will take turns saying A's lines and Group Two will take turns saying B's lines. Switch roles. If someone is not able to say their line, the other group has the chance to say it and earn the point, and vice versa.

IV.   ROLE-PLAYING

How would you say the dialog in the situations below?

A. A is embarrassed to ask; B is very sorry because he doesn't have any money to lend to his friend.

B. A looks worried; B turns his pockets inside out to prove to A that he is not lying.

C. B is obviously annoyed that A is borrowing money from him. A looks offended.

V.   VOCABULARY

Familiarize yourself with the following words that you will need to use in the following sections. Ask your teacher to help you pronounce them correctly.

A. Counting Money

síngko	five centavos
dies	ten centavos
kínse	fifteen centavos
bainte, piséta	twenty centavos
bainte síngko, binting	twenty five centavos
trainta	thirty centavos
kuarénta	forty centavos

223

singkuenta, salapi	fifty centavos
sintábo, sentimo	centavo, one centavo
sisénta	sixty centavos
seténta	seventy centavos
otsénta	eighty centavos
nobénta	ninety centavos

B. Nouns

bangko	bank
búlang	cockfight
dágom	needle
diksionário	dictionary
galiéra	cockpit
kaséro/a	landlord
mákina	machine, sewing machine
matríkula	tuition
páyong	umbrella
pléte	fare
sagaysay	comb
ságot, regálo	gift
sarming	mirror
útang	debt

C. Verbs

1. AG-

agbasbása	going to school, reading
agis-iski	skiing

2. -AN (past tense -IN--AN)

binayádan	paid

3. -UM-

bumisbisíta	visiting

4. MA- (past tense NA-)

naábak	be defeated, lost

5. MANG-

nangábak   defeated someone, won

CHANGING THE DIALOG

A. Using the situations below, and referring to the vocabulary section you have just studied, how would you change:

PART 1 of the dialog?

1. A would like to borrow
$$\begin{cases} \text{twenty dollars.} \\ \text{forty-five dollars.} \\ \text{twenty-seven pesos.} \\ \text{one dollar.} \\ \text{seventy-five cents.} \\ \text{fifty centavos.} \\ \text{twenty-five centavos.} \\ \text{one centavo.} \\ \text{one penny.} \end{cases}$$

PART 2 of the dialog?

1. B says he doesn't have a
$$\begin{cases} \text{car.} \\ \text{dictionary.} \\ \text{watch.} \\ \text{typewriter.} \\ \text{sewing machine.} \\ \text{new pair of shoes.} \\ \text{new pair of pants.} \\ \text{pair of glasses.} \\ \text{needle.} \\ \text{ballpoint pen.} \\ \text{paper.} \\ \text{mirror.} \\ \text{comb.} \\ \text{umbrella.} \end{cases}$$

PART 3 of the dialog?

1. A says he needs the money to
$$\begin{cases} \text{pay his debt.} \\ \text{buy a book.} \\ \text{eat lunch.} \\ \text{buy a present.} \\ \text{go see a movie.} \end{cases}$$

225

2. A says he

{
bought a new pair of glasses.
bought a new watch.
bought a new car.
paid his debt.
paid his tuition.
had a date last night.
took a vacation.
lost at the cockfight.
}

PART 4 of the dialog?

1. B suggests that A
   borrow from

{
his girlfriend.
his landlord.
his boss.
the bank.
}

PART 5 of the dialog?

1. A says his parents
   are in

{
Tahiti.
Spain.
Europe.
China.
Rome.
}

2. A says his
   parents are

{
in Japan, working.
in the Philippines, visiting.
in Colorado, skiing.
in New York, going to
   school.
}

VII.   QUESTION AND ANSWER

Get a partner and practice asking and answering these questions
with him or her. Try asking other questions, too. Ask your teacher
to give you the Ilokano for words you do not know. Speak only in
Ilokano.

1. Ania ti masápol ni A?

2. Mano ti masápol ni A?

3. Adda kadi kuarta ni B?

4. Ápay a masápol ni A ti kuarta?

5. Nagsueldo kadin ni A wenno saan pay?

6. Ápay a naibos ti sueldo ni A?

7. Sinno kano koma ti pagdawátan ni A ti kuarta?

8. Adda kadi da Tátang ni A?

9. Napanan da Tátang ni A?

10. Ania ngata ti aramíden ni A?

VIII. NOTES

A. Grammar

1.

Predicate	Subject
Existential word	Possessed indefinite noun phrase

Awan	kuarta ı k.

In Lesson Twelve we discussed existential sentences with definite and indefinite subjects. Those sentences asserted the existence (or non-existence) of something or some location. However, *adda* and *awan* also are used to assert possession of something by someone. In such sentences these existential words translate as either have or not have:

    a. Adda ások.   I have a dog.

    b. Awan kuartána.   He doesn't have any money.

Both of these sentences can have locative phrases following the subject, like indefinite locative existentials do:

    c. Adda ások idiay balaymi.
        I have a dog at my house.

    d. Awan kuartána iti bolsána.
        He has no money in his pocket.

The only difference between a possessive existential and an indefinite locative existential is that the former must have a possessive pronoun or noun phrase as part of its subject, while these cannot occur with the latter. Compare the following two sentences:

227

e. Adda libro iti rabaw ti lamisáan.
There is a book on top of the table.

f. Adda librok iti rabaw ti lamisáan.
I have a book on top of the table.

IX. EXERCISES

A. Ask questions about the words in italics. Use appropriate question words—*sinno, ania, sadinno, ápay, kaano,* or *mano.*

1. Napan ni *Isabel* idiay pagsiapíngan.

   Sinno ti napan idiay pagsiapíngan?

2. Kaduána ni *Cecilia.*

   _____

3. Gimmátangda ti *katre.*

   _____

4. Nanganda iti *restawran ti Insik.*

   _____

5. *Nagáwidda* iti alas dos.

   _____

6. Simmangpetda idiay balayda iti *alas tres.*

   _____

7. Idi simmangpetda idiay balayda, kinol-ápanda ti *gay-yemda.*

   _____

8. *Binting* ti dináwatna kaniak.

   _____

9. *Naábakda ngamin* isu nga awan kuartáda.

   _____

228

10. Nagbló-awt *da* ta nangábakda.

_____

11. Idi nagsueldo ni Ely, binayádanna ti *útangna.*

_____

B. Examine the models below and use them as a guide in translating the following sentences into Ilokano.

1. Lucas is at the Capitol.
   Adda ni Lucas idiay Kapi-tolio.

2. Lucas has a job at the Capitol.
   Adda trabáho ni Lucas idiay Kapitolio.

3. Merle is not in the red room.
   Awan ni Merle iti nalabbága a siled.

4. Merle does not have a chair in the red room.
   Awan ti tugaw ni Merle iti nalabbága a siled.

5. There is no umbrella.
   Awan ti páyong.

6. She does not have an umbrella.
   Awan ti páyongna.

7. Emilio is in the car.
   _____

8. Sheila does not have a raincoat.
   _____

9. Minda is not at the house.
   _____

10. We have an exam.
   _____

229

11. They don't have any _____

    money. _____

12. The nurses don't have _____

    jobs. _____

13. My Mánong has a new _____

    job. _____

14. The doctor is not in _____

    the office. _____

15. We (you and I) were not _____

    at the meeting. _____

C. Examine the models below and use them as a guide in answering the rest of the questions. Remember that you can substitute a Genitive pronoun (*ko* set) for a Genitive noun phrase (the noun phrase which substitutes for the *ko* set).

> Adda lápis ni Fe?
> Does Fe have a pencil?
>
> Wen, adda lápisna.
> Yes, she has a pencil.

Question

1. Adda kuartam? Wen, adda kuartak.
   Do you have any money? Yes, I have some money.
   (positive response)

2. Adda baro a karro ni Awan, awan ti baro a
   Fely? karróna.
   Does Fely have a new car? No she does not have a
   new car.
   (negative response)

3. Awan ti padaya da Emy?
   Are Emy and her companions
   not having a party?

   Wen, awan ti padayáda.
   Yes, they don't have a
   party.
   (agreeing response)

4. Awan ti libro dagiti
   ubbing?
   Don't the children have
   books?

   Wen, adda libróda.
   Yes, they have books.
   Saan man, adda libróda.
   On the contrary, they
   have books.
   (disagreeing response)

5. Adda kallugong ti lakay?

   _____
   (positive response)

6. Adda sigarilióyo?

   _____
   (negative response)

7. Awan eksámentayo?

   _____
   (agreeing response)

8. Awan ti aramídentayo?

   _____
   (disagreeing response)

9. Awan sapátos ni Daniel?

   _____
   (agreeing response)

10. Awan lisensia ni Miguel?

    _____
    (disagreeing response)

11. Awan ti táo idiay uneg?

    _____
    (agreeing response)

12. Awan idiay uneg ti maestra?

    _____
    (agreeing response)

13. Adda ni Pilíta?

    _____
    (positive response)

14. Adda káma idiay sála?

    _____
    (negative response)

15. Adda makinília ditoy
    opisínayo?

    _____
    (negative response)

X.   COMMUNICATION ACTIVITY

A. Bring pictures to class, showing the interior of rooms in a house. Tell the class what is in the pictures.

B. Bring pictures of two different tourist places. Compare the places and make a decision as to which would be the better place to go.

C. Play the game 'Whosit?' (Parker game #50). All questions and answers are to be in Ilokano only.

D. 1. Read the puzzle.

> Agkaábay da Bitoy ken Mariano. Agkaábay met da Naty ken Marina. Adda ni Marina iti sanguánan ni Bitoy. Adda ni Naty iti sanguánan ni Mariano. Adda ni Maning iti kannawan ni Naty. Adda ni Efren iti kannigid ni Marina. Adda ni Maning iti kannigid ni Mariano. Adda ni Efren Iti kannawan ni Bitoy.

    2. Put the people in their proper places at the dinner table.

    3. Ask your partner questions on the content of the puzzle.

XI.   WRITING PRACTICE

A. Write a detailed summary of the dialog.

B. Write a letter to a friend asking her to lend you something, explaining in detail why you need it. Explain also why you do not have what you are asking for.

Glossary

The glossary contained in the following pages includes some of the main classes of Ilokano words. Many root words can function in more than one class and may be found in more than one place. A number of words listed as nouns and verbs might not be considered to be such in English. However, in Ilokano they function semantically as such. In the pronoun tables, the number 1 refers to first person, or speaker. First person plural is the exclusive pronoun. It does not include the person spoken to. The number 2 refers to the second person, or person spoken to. When singular, the numbers 1 and 2 refer to the dual person, i.e., the speaker and one hearer. When plural, the numbers 1 and 2 refer to the first person inclusive pronoun. It refers not only to the speaker (and his group) but to the hearers. The number 3 refers to the third person, the person or thing that is being spoken about. The symbol ø refers to the absence of any pronoun form, when such an absence can be interpreted as third person singular.

I. PERSONAL PRONOUNS

A. Subject or AK Set

English	Singular	Person	Plural	English
I	-ak	1	-kami	we (exclusive)
you & me	-ta	1,2	-tayo	we (inclusive)
you	-ka	2	-kayo	you
he/she/it	ø, iso, isúna	3	-da	they

B. Genitive or KO Set

English	Singular	Person	Plural	English
I	-ko, -k	1	-mi	we (exclusive)
you & me	-ta	1,2	-tayo	we (inclusive)
you	-mo, -m	2	-yo	you
he/she/it	-na	3	-da	they

233

C. Locative or KANIAK Set*

English	Singular	Person	Plural	English
to me to us you & me to you to him/ her/it	kaniak kadata kenka kenkuána	1 1,2 2 3	kadakami kadatayo kadakayo kadakuáda	to us (exclusive) to us (inclusive) to you to them

*The Locative or *KANIAK* Set can also be translated by prepositions other than 'to', such as 'at' or 'with'.

D. Predicate or SIAK Set

English	Singular	Person	Plural	English
I you & me you he/she/it	siak data sika isu, súna	1 1,2 2 3	dakami datayo dakayo isúda	we (exclusive) we (inclusive) you they

II. DEMONSTRATIVES

A. Subject, Genitive, and Predicate

	Singular	Plural
this	daytoy	dagitoy
that, near	dayta	dagita
that, far	daydiay	dagidiay
that, recent	daytay	dagitay
that, long ago	daydi	dagidi

B. Locative

	Singular	Plural
this	kadaytoy	kadagitoy
that, near	kadayta	kadagita
that, far	kadaydiay	kadagidiay
that, recent	kadaytay	kadagitay
that, long ago	kadaydi	kadagidi

234

III. LOCATIVE WORDS

here	ditoy
there, near	dita
there, far	idiay

IV. TIME WORDS

now, today	itatta, ita
before, today	itattay, itay
before, earlier than today	idi

V. DETERMINERS

A. Subject, Genitive, and Predicate

		Singular	Plural
Common Noun	(general)	ti	dagiti
	this	toy	
	that, near	ta	
	that, far	diay	
	that, recent	tay	
	that, long ago	di	
Personal Noun		ni	da

B. Locative

	Singular	Plural
Common Noun	iti	kadagiti
Personal Noun	kenni	kada

235

VI.   SPANISH NUMERALS

úno	1	katórse	14	seténta	70
dos	2	kínse	15	otsénta	80
tres	3	disisais	16	nobénta	90
kuatro	4	disisiéte	17	sien, siénto	100
síngko	5	disiótso	18	dos siéntos	200
sais	6	disinuébe	19	tres siéntos	300
siéte	7	bainte	20	kuatro siéntos	400
otso	8	bainte-úno	21	kiniéntos	500
nuébe	9	bainte-dos	22	sais siéntos	600
dies	10	trainta	30	siete siéntos	700
ónse	11	kuarénta	40	otso siéntos	800
dóse	12	singkuénta	50	nuebe siéntos	900
tráse	13	sisénta	60	mil	1000

VII.   ILOKANO NUMERALS

maysa	1	sangapúlo ket dua	12
dua	2	duapúlo	20
tallo	3	tallupúlo	30
uppat	4	uppat a púlo	40
lima	5	limapúlo	50
innem	6	innem a púlo	60
pito	7	pitupúlo	70
walo	8	walupúlo	80
siam	9	siam a púlo	90
sangapúlo	10	sangagasot	100
sangapúlo ket maysa	11	sangaríbo	1000

VIII. QUESTION WORDS

from where	taga-ano	when	kaano
how	kasano	where	sadinno
how (greeting)	kumusta	where at	ayan
how many	mano	who	sinno
how related	kapin-ano	why	ápay
what	ania	how much each	sagmamano

IX. SENTENCE MODIFIERS

according to someone	kano	please	man
		still	pay
again	manen	so (discovery, realization)	gáyam
also	met		
just	láeng	then	ngarod
maybe	sigúro	too	met
moreover	pay	very	únay
perhaps	ngata	yet	pay

X. CONJUNCTIONS

and	ket	so that	tapno
and	ken	that's why	iso nga
because	ta	until	aginggána
but	ngem	when (future)	no
even	úray no	when (recent past)	itay
if	no		
might	baka, amangan	when (remote past)	idi
or	wenno		

XI. TERMS OF ADDRESS

aunt	nána	grandmother	lélang
brother, older	mánong	grandparent	ápong
		lady, my young	balásangko
child, my	nakkong		
father	tátang	madam	ápo
grandfather	lélong		

man, my	barok	sir	ápo
young		sister,	mánang
mother	nánang	older	
sibling,	áding	uncle	táta
younger			

XII. KINSHIP TERMS

aunt	íkit
brother-in-law	káyong
brother or sister	kabsat
cousin	kasinsin
father	ama
grandfather	lélong
grandmother	lélang
grandparent	ápong
husband	mister, lakay
mother	ina
nephew, niece	kaanakan
offspring	anak
parent-in-law	katugángan
parent of one's child's spouse	abalayan
parents	dadakkel, nagannak
second cousin	kapidua
sister-in-law	ípag
son/daughter-in-law	manúgang
spouse	asáwa
spouse of the sibling of one's spouse	abírat
third cousin	kapitlo
uncle	uliteg
wife	mísis, baket

XIII. ADJECTIVES

absent- minded	kábaw
affectionate	naayat, nadungngo
afraid	mabuteng
arrogant	natangsit
bad	madi
bald	kalbo
beautiful	napintas
big	dakkel
bitter	napait
bland	nasabeng
bright	nalaing
cheap	nalaka
clean	nadalos
clear	nalitnaw
clever	nalaing
cold	nalamíis
cranky	naunget
deaf	túleng
difficult	narígat
diligent	nagaget
dirty	narugit
dry	namaga
dusty	natápok
embarrassed	mabain
embarrassing	nakabábain
expensive	nangína
fair (skinned)	napúdaw
far	adayo
fast	napardas
fat	nataba, nalukmeg
few	bassit
filthy	dugyot, nadugyot

fine	nasayáat
fragrant	nabanglo
funny	nakakatkatáwa
good	naimbag
good	nalaing, mayat
green (unripe)	naáta
gross	bastos
handsome	naguápo, nataráki
happy	naragsak
hard	natangken
healthy	nasalun-at
hot	napúdot
humble	nanumo
hungry	mabisin
industrious	nagaget
intelligent	nasírib
joyous	narambak
kind	nasingpet
lazy	nasadot
liar	ulbod, naulbod
little	bassit
long	atiddog
loose	naláwa
lost	napúkaw
many	ado
much	ado
narrow	akíkid
near	asideg
nearly	nganngáni
new	baro
noisy	natagari, naringgor
odorous	nabangsit

old	dáan
old (rice)	báak
organized	naurnos
painful	nasakit
patient	naános
poor	napanglaw, napobre
pretty	napintas
proud	natangsit
puckery	nasugpet
quiet	naulímek
rich	nabaknang
ripe	naluom
rude	bastos
salty	naapgad
scary	nakabutbuteng
short (person)	pandek
short	ababa
shortly	mabiit
shy	mabain
sick	masakit
skinny	nakuttong
slow	naináyad
small	bassit
smelly	naángot
smokey	naasok
smooth	nalamúyot
soft	nalukneng
sour	naalsem
spicy hot	nagásang
strict	istrikto
strong	napigsa
sturdy	nalagda
sweet	nasam-it

talkative	tarabítab
tall	natáyag
tasty	naímas
tender	naganos
thick	napuskol
thin	naingpis
tidy	naurnos
tight	nailet
tired	nabannog
tough	natangken
troublesome	nalóko
ugly	naalas, naláad
weak	nakapsot
well	naimbag, nasayáat
wet	nabasa
wide	akába

XIV. NOUNS

adult	nataengan
afternoon	malem
airplane	eropláno
arm	takiag
armpit	kilikíli
assignment	asáynmen
aunt	íkit
bagoong	buggúong
ballpoint pen	bolpen
banana	saba
bank	bangko
bathroom	banio
bed	káma, katre
beer	bir, serbésa

belief	pammáti
bell	kampána
belt	sinturon
bicycle	bisikléta
bird	billit
bittermelon	paria
blackboard	pisarra
blanket	ules
blouse	blúsa
body	bagi
bone	tulang
book	libro
boss	bos
boyfriend	nóbio
bracelet	pulséra
breakfast	pamigat
breast	súso
brother	kabsat
brother-in-law	káyong
building	pasdek
cabinet, portable	aparador
cafeteria	kapiteria, kantína
candy	dulse
car	karro
cashier	kahéra
cat	púsa
chair	tugaw
cheek	pingping
cheese	késo
chest	barúkong
chicken	manok

child	ubing, anak
chin	tímid
church	simbáan
cigarette	sigarilio
city	siudad
class	kláse
clothes	bádo
cockfight	búlang, sábong
cockroach	ípes
coconut	niog
coffee	kape
comb	sagaysay
companion	kadua
cook	kusinéro/a
country	pagilian
cousin, first	kasinsin
cousin, second	kapidua
cousin, third	kapitlo
co-worker	katrabahuan
crackers	biskwit
curtain	kortína
daughter-in-law	manúgang
day	aldaw
debt	útang
dentist	dentista
dinner	pangrabii
doctor	doktor
dollar	doliar
door	rídaw, puerta
drainage canal	estéro
dress	bestído, bádo

drink	inumen, mainom
drunkard	bartikéro
ear	lapáyag
earrings	arítos
egg	itlog
elbow	síko
engineer	inhiniéro
evening	rabii
exam	eksámen
eye	mata
eyebrow	kíday
eyeglasses	antiparra, antióhos
eyelash	kurimatmat
face	rúpa
family	pamilia
fare	pléte
father	ama
female	babái
filmstar	artista
finger	rámay
fingernail	kuko
fire	apoy
fish	ikan
fish sauce	patis
flower	sábong
fly (insect)	ngílaw
food	kanen, makan
foot	sáka
forehead	múging
friend	gayyem
front	sanguánan
fruit	prútas
garage	garáhe

garbage	basúra
gift	ságot, regálo
ghost	al-alia, bánig
girlfriend	nóbia
glass	sarming
glass, drinking	báso
grandchild	apo
grass	rúot
guava	bayábas
guest	bisíta, sangaíli
guitar	gitára
hair	buok
half (hour)	média
hammock	indáyon
hand	íma
handkerchief	panyo
head	úlo
heart	púso
hat	kallugong
home	balay
hour	óras
house	balay
house ladder	agdan
ice	yélo
ice cream	sorbéte
jewelry	aláhas
kitchen	kusína
lady, young	balásang
landlord	kaséro/a
lawyer	abogádo/a
leg	gúrong
letter	súrat

library	laybrari
light	sílaw
lips	bibig
living room	sálas
lunch	pangaldaw
magazine	mágasin
male	laláki
man, young	baro
mango	mangga
market	tiendáan
mat, sleep- ing	ikamen
matches	posporo
mattress	kotson
mayor	mayor
meat	karne
meeting	míting
mestizo	mestíso
midday	aldaw
milk	gátas
minute	minúto
mirror	sarming
money	kuarta
month	búlan
morning	bigat
mosquito	lamok
mosquito net	moskitéro
mother	ina
mountain	bantay
mouth	ngíwat
movie	síne
nail	lansa
name	nágan
neck	tengnged

necklace	kuentas
needle	dágom
neighbor	kaarrúba
nephew	kaanakan
newspaper	diario, pagiwarnak
niece	kaanakan
night	rabii
nose	agong
nurse	nars
ocean	baybay
office	opisína
offspring	anak
others	daddúma
outside	ruar
pajama	padiáma
pants	pantalon
paper	papel
parent-in-law	katugángan
parents	dadakkel, nagannak
parking lot	pagparadáan, pagparkíngan
part-time	partaym
party	padaya
peanuts	mani
pencil	lápis
person	táo
picture	ladáwan
pillow	pungan
place	lugar
plant, ornamental	masétas
plate	pinggan, pláto
pocket	bolsa

police	pulis
practice	praktis
president	presidente
principal	prinsipal
program	prográma
province	probinsia
rain	túdo
rear	likudan
record album	pláka
refrigerator	aysbaks
rice	bagas
rice cake	kankanen
rice (cooked)	innapoy
riddle	burburtia
ring	singsing
river	karayan
room	siled, kuarto
rope	tali
rose	rósas
salary	sueldo
salt	asin
salted seeds	tsampoy
school	eskuéla
sea	baybay
secretary	sekretaria
shawl	kagay
shirt, short- sleeved	pólo
shoes	sapátos
shorts	korto
shoulder	abága
sibling	kabsat
sink	labábo
sister	kabsat (a babái)

sister-in-law	ípag
skin	kúdil
skirt	palda
sky	lángit
slippers	sinílas
socks	medias
son-in-law	manúgang
spouse	asáwa
state	estádo
stone	bato
stove	dalikan
store	tiangge
stream	wáig
student	estudiante
student, fellow	kaeskueláan
sugar	asúkar
suitcase	maléta
sun	ínit
surname	apelyído
swing	indáyon
table	lamisáan
tea	itsa
teacher (female)	maestra
teacher (male)	maestro
teeth	ngípen
things (one uses)	alikámen
time	óras, tiempo
tongue	díla
toothbrush	sipilio

top	rabaw
towel	tualia
town	íli
tree	káyo
trousers	pantalon
trunk	baol
truth	pudno
tuition	matríkula
umbrella	páyong
uncle	uliteg
undershirt	kamiséta
university	unibersidad
vegetable	nateng
vehicle	lúgan
village	bario
vinegar	suka
visitor	bisíta, sangaíli
voice	tímek
volcano	bulkáno
waist	síket
watch (wrist)	relo
water	danom
water buffalo	nuang
weather	tiempo
week	láwas
wife	baket, asáwa
window	táwa, bentána
woman, old	baket
work	trabáho
world	lúbong
year	tawen
yesterday	kalman

XV.   VERBS

accompany	kúyog,
	mangkúyog,
	kuyúgen
acquainted,	am-ammo,
be	agam-ammo,
	am-ammuen,
	mangiyam-ammo
answer	sungbat,
	agsungbat,
	sumungbat,
	mangsungbat,
	sungbátan
apply makeup	méykap,
	agméykap,
	mangméykap,
	meykápan
arrive	sangpet,
	agsangpet,
	sumangpet,
	mangisangpet,
	sangpetan
ask (question)	saludsod,
	agsaludsod,
	mangsaludsod,
	saludsúden
ask for	dáwat,
	agdáwat,
	dumáwat,
	mangdáwat,
	dawáten,
	idáwat,
	dawátan
bang into	dungpar,
	agdungpar,
	dumungpar,
	mangdungpar,
	dungpáren,
	idungpar

bath, take a	dígos, agdígos, mangdígos, digusen
believe	páti, mamáti, patien
born	anak, maiyanak
born, be	anak, maiyanak, iyanak
borrow	búlod, agbúlod, bumúlod, mangbúlod, bulúden, bulúdan
borrow (money)	útang, agútang, umútang, mangútang, utángen, utángan
break	búong, bumúong, mangbúong, buúngen
bring	yeg, agiyeg, mangiyeg, iyeg
brush, teeth	sipilio, agsipilio, mangsipilio, sipiliuwen
burnt, be	kesset, makset

buy	gátang, aggatang, gumátang, manggátang, gatángen
call	ayab, agayab, mangayab, ayaban
call up	kol-ap, agkol-ap, mangkol-ap, kol-ápan
call up	awag, agáwag, umáwag, mangáwag, awágan
chew	ngalngal, agngalngal, mangngalngal, ngalngálen
choose	píli, agpíli, pumíli, mangpíli, pilien
climb	úli, agúli, umúli, mangiyúli, ulien
clean	dalos, agdalos, mangdalos, dalusan
close	rikep, agrikep, rumikep,

	mangirikep,
	irikep
comb hair	sagaysay,
	agsagaysay,
	mangsagaysay,
	sagaysáyen
come	umay,
	umayan
come up	úli,
	agúli,
	umúli,
	ulien
cook	lúto,
	aglúto,
	manglúto,
	lutuen,
	ilúto
count	bílang,
	agbílang,
	bumílang,
	mangbílang,
	bilángen,
	bilángan
cry	sángit,
	agsángit,
	sumángit,
	isángit,
	sangítan
cut off	púted,
	agpúted,
	pumúted,
	mangpúted,
	putden,
	putdan
cut (with	kartib,
scissors)	agkartib,
	mangkartib,
	kartíben,
	kartíban

dance	sála, agsála, sumála, mangisála, saláen, isála, saláan
defeated, be	ábak, maábak
defeat someone	ábak, mangábak, abáken
destroy	dadáel, agdadáel, mangdadáel, dadaélen
dip into	sawsaw, agsawsaw, sumawsaw, mangisawsaw, isawsaw, sawsáwan
dizzy	úlaw, mangúlaw, maúlaw, uláwen
do	arámid, agarámid, mangarámid, aramíden
dress	bádo, agbádo, mangbádo, baduan
drink	inom, aginom, uminom, inumen, inuman

eat	kan, mangan, kanen
enter	serrek, agserrek, sumrek, mangiserrek, serken, iserrek, serkan
exercise	watwat, agwatwat, watwáten
explain	palawag, agpalawag, mangipalawag, ipalawag
explode	bettak, agbettak, bumtak, mangbettak, bettaken
fill	punno, mangpunno, mapno, punuen
finish	leppas, agleppas, mangleppas, malpas, leppasen
fold	kupin, agkupin, mangkupin, kupinen
follow	saruno, agsaruno, sumaruno, mangsaruno,

	mangisaruno,
	sarunuen,
	isaruno
get	ála,
	agála,
	mangála,
	aláen,
	aláan
get down	baba,
	agbaba,
	bumaba,
	mangibaba,
	ibaba,
	babaan
give	ited,
	agited,
	mangted,
	itden,
	ited,
	ikkan
go	pan,
	mapan
go along	kúyog,
	kumúyog
go home	áwid,
	agáwid,
	awídan (to)
go together	kúyog,
	agkúyog
go to school	bása,
	agbása
go to school	eskuéla,
	ageskuéla
go out	ruar,
	rumuar,
	ruaren,
	iruar,
	ruaran

hang clothes on the line	balaybay, agibalaybay, mangibalaybay, ibalaybay
happen	pasámak, mapasámak
have a snack	merienda, agmerienda, meriendáen
hear	dengngeg, agdengngeg, dumngeg, mangdengngeg, denggen
help	túlong, tumúlong, mangtúlong, itúlong, tulóngan
hit	kábil, agkábil, kumábil, mangkábil, kabílen
hurry	apura, agapura, apuraen
inquire	saludsod, agsaludsod, mangsaludsod, saludsúden
invite	áwis, agáwis, mangáwis, awísen
jump	lagto, aglagto, lumagto, mangilagto,

	ilagto, lagtuen
kill	patay, pumatay, mangpatay, patayen
kill (for food)	parti, agparti, pumarti, mangparti, partien
know	ammo, agammo, mangammo, ammuen
laugh	katáwa, agkatáwa, katawáan
laundry, do	laba, aglaba, mangilaba, labaan
learn	sursúro, agsursúro, sursuruen
leave	panaw, agpanaw, pumánaw, panáwan
lie down	idda, agidda, umidda, iddaan
lie on stomach	kelleb, kumleb
lie, tell a	ulbod, agulbod
like	gusto, gumusto,

	gustuen, magustuan
listen	dengngeg, agdengngeg, dumngeg, denggen
look at	kíta, kumíta, mangkíta, kitáen
look for	sápol, agsápol, sumápol, mangsápol, sapúlen
love	ayat, agayat, mangayat, ayaten
make	arámid, agarámid, mangarámid, aramíden
melt	rúnaw, mangrúnaw, runáwen
none	awan, agawan, umawan
nothing	awan
open	lukat, aglukat, lumukat, manglukat, ilukat, lukatan
party, have a	daya, agdaya, agpadaya

pass	áwat, agiyáwat, mangiyáwat, iyáwat
pay	báyad, agbáyad, bumáyad, mangbáyad, bayádan
peel	ukis, agukis, mangukis, ukisan
pick	puros, agpuros, pumuros, mangpuros, purusen, purusan
pick up	pídot, agpídot, pumídot, mangpídot, pidúten, pidútan
pick up (lift)	bagkat, agbagkat, bumagkat, mangbagkat, bagkáten
play (game)	ay-áyam, agay-áyam, ay-ayámen
play (instru- ment)	tokar, agtokar, tokaren, tokaran
prepare	sagána, agsagána,

	mangiságana, isagána
put	kábil, agikábil, mangikábil, ikábil, kabílan
put away	dúlin, agidúlin, mangidúlin, idúlin
quarrel	ápa, agápa, apáen
rain	túdo, agtúdo
receive	áwat, agáwat, umáwat, mangáwat, awáten
read	bása, agbása, bumása, mangbása, basáen, basáan
remember	lagip, lumagip, manglagip, lagipen
remove	ikkat, agikkat, umikkat, mangikkat, ikkaten, ikkatan
rest, take a	inana, aginana

return	subli, agsubli, sumubli, mangisubli, sublien, isubli, sublian
ride	lúgan, aglúgan, lumúgan, mangilúgan, ilúgan, lugánan
rotten, be	lungsot, malungsot, lungsúten
satisfied (with food), be	bussog, mabsog
satisfy (with food) someone	bussog, mangbussog, bussugen
say	kuna, agkuna, kunaen
see	kíta, agkíta, kumíta, mangkíta, kitáen
sell	láko, agláko, lumáko, mangiláko, iláko, lakuan
send	paw-it, agpaw-it, mangipaw-it, ipaw-it, paw-ítan

serenade	tapat,
	agtapat,
	mangtapat,
	tapatan
sew	dáit,
	agdáit,
	dumáit,
	mangdáit,
	daíten,
	daítan
shampoo hair	gulgol,
	aggulgol,
	manggulgol,
	gulgúlan
shopping, go	siáping,
	agsiaping
shout	pukkaw,
	agpukkaw,
	pumukkaw,
	mangipukkaw,
	pukkawan
sing	kanta,
	agkanta,
	kumanta,
	mangkanta,
	kantáen,
	kantáan
sit	tugaw,
	agtugaw,
	tumugaw,
	mangitugaw,
	itugaw,
	tugawan
sleep	túrog,
	matúrog,
	turúgan
slice	íwa,
	agíwa,
	umíwa,
	mangíwa,

	iwáen, iwáan
smile	ísem, agísem, umísem, isman
speak	sao, agsao, sumao, sawen/saw-en
spit	tupra, agtupra, tumupra, mangitupra, itupra, tupráan
stain	mantsa, agmantsa, mangmantsa, mantsáan
stand	takder, agtakder, tumakder, mangitakder, itakder, takderan
step on	baddek, agbaddek, bumaddek, mangbaddek, ibaddek, baddekan
startle	kelláat, mangkelláat, makláat (be startled), kellaáten
stay	gian, aggian
stay overnight	yan, umian

stop	sardeng, agsardeng, sumardeng, mangisardeng, isardeng, sardengan
stroll, go for	pasiar, agpasiar, pumasiar, pasiaran
study	ádal, agádal, adálen
surprised, be	seddáaw, masdáaw
swallow	tilmon, agtilmon, tumilmon, mangtilmon, tilmúnen
sweep	ságad, agságad, mangságad, sagádan
swim	dígos, agdígos, mangdígos, digósen
take to	pan, mangipan, ipan
take along	kúyog, mangikúyog, ikúyog
take care of	aywan, agaywan, mangaywan, aywánan

267

taste	raman, agraman, rumaman, mangraman, ramanan
tear	pígis, pumígis, mangpígis, pigísen, pigísan
tell	baga, agibaga, mangibaga, ibaga
test, take a	tes, agtes
test, take a	eksámen, ageksámen
there is	adda, agadda, addaan
thirsty	uwaw, manguwaw, mauwaw, uwawen
throw out	belleng, agibelleng, mangibelleng, ibelleng
toot a horn	busína, agbusína, bumusína, busináan
transfer	ákar, agákar, umákar, mangiyákar, iyákar, akáran

turn off light	iddep, agiddep, mangiddep, iddepen
type	makinília, agmakinília, mangmakinília, makiniliáen
use up	ibos, mangibos, ibusen, ibusan
visit	bisíta, agbisíta, bumisíta, mangbisíta, bisitáen
visit	sarungkar, sumarungkar, mangsarungkar, sarungkáran
wait	úray, agúray, mangúray, uráyen
wash (dishes)	innaw, aginnaw, manginnaw, innáwan
wash (face)	diram-os, agdiram-os, diram-úsan
wash	úgas, agúgas, mangúgas, ugásan
wash	buggo, agbuggo, mangbuggo, bugguan

watch	búya,
	agbúya,
	mangbúya,
	buyáen
weave, cloth	abel,
	agabel,
	mangabel,
	ablen
whisper	arasáas,
	mangiyarasáas,
	iyarasáas,
	arasaásan
wipe	púnas,
	agpúnas,
	mangpúnas,
	punásan
write	súrat,
	agsúrat,
	sumúrat,
	mangsúrat,
	suráten,
	surátan

XVI. PSEUDO-VERBS

can	balin,
	mabalin
like	ayat,
	mayat,
	kayat
necessary, be	sápol,
	masápol
no	saan
possible, be	balin,
	mabalin
want	ayat,
	mayat,
	kayat,
	kayaten

270

XVII. ADVERBS

above	ngáto
afterwards	kalpasanna
all	ámin
always	kanáyon
before	itattay (recent), idi (remote)
behind	likudan
below	baba
beside	ábay
between	baet, nagbaetan
edge	ígid
every	káda
immediately	dágos
in front of	sangúanan
inside	uneg
later	madamdama
left	kannigid
middle	tengnga
now	ita
often	masansan
once in a while	sagpaminsan
on top	rabaw
rarely	manmano
right	kannawan
side	sikigan
sometimes	pasaray, no daddúma, no maminsan
today	ita, itatta
tomorrow	intuno bigat
underneath	sírok

Appendix One

I. FREE TRANSLATIONS OF DIALOGS
Lesson One

   A: Good morning, Miss.

   B: Good morning to you.

   A: What is your name?

   B: Luz.

   A: What is your surname?

   B: Ulep.

   A: Really? Oh, Ulep is my mother's surname also!

   B: Is that so? What's your name?

Lesson Two

   A: Where do you come from?

   B: I'm from Kalihi.

   A: Where in Kalihi?

   B: Kalihi-Uka.

   A: Where do you stay now?

   B: (There) in Kalihi also.

   A: Do you work?

   B: Yes, but only part-time.

   A: Where are you going now?

   B: I'm going to work.

   A: Goodbye then.

   B: Okay.

Lesson Three

A: Do you know each other?

B: No, we don't know each other.

A: Lino, this is Lisa. She is my cousin. Lisa, this is Lino. He is my classmate in History.

B: How are you, Lisa?

C: I'm fine and you?

B: I'm fine.

C: Are you from here?

B: No, I'm from Maui.

C: Oh, I'm from Maui, too!

B: Is that so? Where in Maui?

Lesson Four

A: Are you Chinese?

B: No, I am American, Spanish, and Filipino.

A: Who is Spanish in your family?

B: My mother. Her surname is Spanish.

A: What is her surname?

B: Enriquez.

A: Oh, so you're a mestizo then!

B: Yes, I'm a mestizo.

A: Who is American in your family?

8: I am. I was born here.

A: Is that so?

Lesson Five

A: Who is your mathematics teacher?

B: Mr. Lucas.

A: Oh, I like Mr. Lucas. He's sharp and he's kind, too.

B: So do I, I like him, too.

A: Why?

B: (Of course), because he is very strict, but he is funny.

A: Oh, what's the time?

B: It's now 2:30.

A: Oh, it's already time for my class!

B: What time is your class?

A: It's 2:30. I've got to go because I'm late.

B: Go now, then.

A: Okay, goodbye then.

B: 'Bye.

Lesson Six

A: Hi, Pari, how are you?

B: Fine, Pari, and you?

A: I'm fine too.

B: Okay, see you.

A: Why are you hurrying?

B: I'm going to work.

A: Where do you work?

B: Downtown. Okay, goodbye.

A: You want to go have a snack?

B: I can't; I'm working. Okay, 'bye, I'm late.

A: Wait a minute! What are you doing tomorrow morning?

Lesson Seven

A: Hello.

B: Lisa, this is Lino, Bert's friend.

A: Which friend of Bert's?

B: His classmate in History.

A: Ah, yes, now I remember.

B: What are you doing on Saturday night?

A: Nothing. I'm not doing anything.

B: Would you like to go to a movie?

A: What movie will we go to see?

B: "Gone With the Wind." Let's go at eight o'clock, okay?

A: Can I bring my little sister?

B: Y-y-yes. You can.

Lesson Eight

A: Anybody home?

B: Come in . . . Oh, Caridad, it's you!

A: What are you doing?

B: Eating mango.

A: Are you eating green mango?

C: Yes, it's good. Here, eat some. Taste it.

A: I don't like green mango. It's very sour.

C: This one isn't too sour.

A: Let me taste it then. Just a little.

B: Here would you like some *bagoong?*

A: Yes, I would, but just a little . . . Wow, green mango with *bagoong* is really tasty!

C: Here, have some more.

Lesson Nine

A: Gee, I feel so sleepy!

B: Why, didn't you sleep last night?

A: I slept, but just a little because we went to meet Burcio's uncle at daybreak.

B: Why, where did he come from?

A: The Philippines. It was already three o'clock when he arrived. And then we went to their house.

B: What did you do there?

A: We ate *balut* and then we drank beer. I ate so many *balut!*

B: How many did you eat?

A: Seven.

B: Seven! You really eat *balut?*

A: Of course. Why, don't you like *balut?*

B: No way, they look gross.

Lesson Ten

A: How was your class today?

B: Fine, Dad.

A: What did you do in school today?

B: We read, then we wrote, then we went to the library, then we ate at the cafeteria . . . we did a lot. It's the same thing everyday.

A: Who was your companion?

B: My schoolmates.

A: Where did you go?

B: To school, Dad.

A: Tell the truth!

B: I didn't go anywhere! You can ask Esteban.

A: Why did your principal call up here then? He was inquiring about you.

Lesson Eleven

A: Have you already finished your homework?

B: Not yet, Dad.

A: Stop that and go study. Turn the TV off.

B: In a little while, Dad. It's almost finished.

A: Turn that TV off, I said!

B: In a little while. I have to watch this because . . .

A: Finish your work, then you can watch TV!

B: Dad, I have to watch this!

A: Why, what is it that you're watching, anyway?

Lesson Twelve

A: Where is my book that was here before?

B: Look there on top of the table.

A: But it's not here.

B: Look in the room there, because you were reading it there last night.

A: It's not there. I already looked for it there.

B: It's probably there, underneath the bed.

A: It's not there. I already looked for it there.

B: Oh, go and see if it's beside the chair, because I think I saw it there before.

A: Oh, yes, that's right!

Lesson Thirteen

A: Why are you moving again?

B: Because it is very noisy at our place.

A: Why is it noisy there?

B: Because it is close to the school. The children really make a racket. Another thing, it is also near the parking lot.

A: It'll be noisier in the place you're moving into, because it is near the freeway.

B: Never mind, because it has air conditioning. If you close the window and turn on the air conditioner, you can't hear the noise outside anymore.

A: Oh, gee, it uses so much electricity.

Lesson Fourteen

A: What is the most beautiful place in the Philippines?

B: Why, are you going to take a vacation?

A: Yes.

B: When are you taking your vacation?

A: In December, because the weather will be fine.

B: There are many beautiful places there but I don't know which is the most beautiful.

A: Never mind. I'll just go with a tour.

B: When is the tour leaving?

A: On the fifteenth of December.

B: Oh, it's a long time yet.

Lesson Fifteen

A: Do you have any money?

B: How much do you need?

A: Ten dollars, if you could lend me that much.

B: Oh, I don't have ten dollars. Why do you need the money?

A: It's because I have a date.

B: Why, didn't you get paid yet?

A: I did, but I bought myself new shoes and pants yesterday. My pay is all gone.

B: Ask your parents.

A: I would, but my parents are not here.

B: Why, where are they?

A: They're in the Ilocos. They're on vacation.

B: Oh, that's too bad! What are you going to do, then?

II.   TRANSLATIONS OF QUESTIONS FROM
       SECTION VII OF EACH LESSON

Lesson One

1. What is B's name?

2. What is B's surname?

3. What is the surname of B's mother?

Lesson Two

1. Where does A come from?

2. Where does A come from in Kalihi?

3. Where does A live?

4. Does A go to work?

5. Where is A going?

Lesson Three

1. Are A and C acquainted with each other?

2. Who is Lisa?

3. Who is Lino?

4. Who is A?

5. Where do Lisa and Lino come from?

6. Is Lisa A's neighbor?

7. Is A Lino's classmate?

8. Are A and Lino siblings?

9. How are A and Lisa related?

10. How about Lino and Lisa, how are they related?

Lesson Four

1. Is B Chinese?

2. What is B?

3. Is the surname of B's mother American?

4. Is B's father's surname American?

5. Who is the mestizo?

6. Who is the American?

7. Who is the Filipino?

8. Why is B an American?

Lesson Five

1. Who is B's teacher in Mathematics?

2. Who is Mr. Lucas?

3. Who likes Mr. Lucas?

4. Why do A and B like Mr. Lucas?

5. What time is A's class?

6. Where is A going?

7. Why is A hurrying?

Lesson Six

1. Why is B hurrying?

2. Where does B work?

3. What does A want to do?

4. Why cannot B go and have a snack?

Lesson Seven

1. Who is calling Lisa?

2. Who is Lino?

3. Who is Lino's fellow student?

4. Is Lino Lisa's fellow student?

5. Is Lino Bert's fellow student in Mathematics?

6. Why is Lino calling Lisa?

7. What is Lisa doing on the following Saturday?

8. What does Lino want to do?

9. What does Lino want to see?

10. What time does Lino want them to go to the movie?

11. Who does Lisa want to take along?

Lesson Eight

1. Who arrived?

2. What are B and C doing?

3. What kind of mangoes are B and C eating?

4. Why doesn't A like green mangoes?

5. Did A taste the green mangoes?

6. What else did they eat?

7. What did they dip the mango into?

8. Did A like green mango with *bagoong?*

9. Do you like green mango with *bagoong?*

10. What are the foods you do not like?

11. What foods are very sour?

Lesson Nine

1. Who is sleepy?

2. Why wasn't B able to sleep on the previous evening?

3. Where did Burcio's uncle come from?

4. What was the time when Burcio's uncle arrived?

5. Where else did A and the others go?

6. What did A and his friends do at Burcio's uncle's place?

7. How many *balut* did A eat?

8. Does A like *balut?*

9. Why doesn't B like *balut?*

10. What about you, do you like *balut?*

11. What things don't you like to eat?

Lesson Ten

1. According to B, how was his class that day?

2. According to B, what did B and his classmates do in school that day?

3. According to B, who were his companions that day?

4. Where did B say they went?

5. Who was said to have made the call to B's house?

6. Who did it say the principal inquired about?

7. Why did B seem to be afraid?

8. Why did B's father seem to be angry?

Lesson Eleven

1. Has B finished his homework?

2. What does A want B to do?

3. What does A want B to turn off?

4. What is said to be almost finished?

5. What does B need to watch?

6. What does A want B to finish before watching TV?

7. Why do you think it is necessary for B to watch the program on TV?

8. What do you think B is watching?

Lesson Twelve

1. What is A looking for?

2. Is A's book on top of the table?

3. What is said that A was doing on the previous evening?

4. Is A's book in the room?

5. Is A's book underneath the bed?

6. According to B, where did she see A's book?

7. Where is A's book?

8. Why do you think A's book is beside the chair?

Lesson Thirteen

1. What is A asking B?

2. Why, is it said, B and his companions are moving?

3. Why, is it said, it is noisy at B's place?

4. Why, is it said, it is noisier where B and his companions are moving to?

5. What, is it said, are B and his companions going to do so they don't hear the noise outside?

6. And you, do you like a house with air conditioning? Why? Why not?

7. Would you like to live close to a freeway? Why? Why not?

Lesson Fourteen

1. What is A inquiring about from B?

2. What is A going to do?

3. When is A going to take his vacation?

4. Why does A want to take his vacation in December?

5. Does B know which is the most beautiful place in the Philippines?

6. What will A do in the Philippines so that he will be able to see the beautiful places there?

7. When will A leave?

8. Is A close to leaving?

Lesson Fifteen

1. What does A need?

2. How much does A need?

3. Does B have any money?

4. Why does A need money?

5. Has A already been paid, or not yet?

6. Why is A's pay all gone?

284

7. Who, is said, should be the ones that A should ask money from?

8. Are A's parents there?

9. Where did A's parents go?

10. What do you think A will do?

III. TRANSLATIONS OF LISTENING PRACTICE
FROM SECTION XII

Lesson Three

Luna is from the Ilocos. His friend is also from the Ilocos. His friend's name is Pablo. They are classmates at McKinley High School.

Pablo lives in Waialua. That is where Luna lives too. They are neighbors in Waialua.

Pablo and Luna do not work together. Pablo works at Dole Pineapple Company. Luna does not go to work.

Pablo and Luna were born in Vigan. That is also where their parents were born.

Pablo and Luna's parents know each other.

Lesson Ten

The Thieves

The car stopped in front of the house. Three men got out. They went to the back of the house. They broke the window of one of the rooms. Afterwards, they climbed through the window.

They got the jewelry and money that were in the closet. They also got the television and other things inside the house. After that, they got into their car and left.

When the family who lived in the house arrived home, they called the police. Two policemen arrived and asked what happened.

Lesson Fourteen

Our Party

Last week, our Ilokano class had a party. That was the best party we've had this year. Mila and Lisa played the piano and they also sang. Mila was better at playing, but Lisa had the better voice. Rosa also played the guitar.

There was a lot of tasty food at the party. Efren brought two kinds of *pinakbet,* one with meat, and the other without. The one with meat was tastier because I like pork.

We also roasted a pig. We chose the smallest pig at the Waialua Piggery because it was the cheapest.

We danced until two o'clock in the morning. We went home at three.

Appendix Two

A. 'Panagorder iti Restawran'
    'Ordering in a Restaurant'

Weytres:	Ania ti kayatyo a kanen, Mánong?	What do you want to eat, Mánong?
Lito:	Daytoy man pinakbet, pansit, laúya, ken adóbo, Áding.	This *pinakbet,* noodles, stew, and *adóbo,* please, Áding.
Weytres:	Adóbo nga ania?	What kind of adóbo?
Lito:	Ket adóbo, a!	*Adóbo,* what else!
Weytres:	Adóbo a báboy wenno adóbo a manok?	Pork *adóbo,* or chicken *adóbo?*
Lito:	Ay, dispensárem, Áding. Adóbo a báboy man.	Sorry, Áding. Pork *adóbo.*
Weytres:	Laúya a báboy wenno báka, Mánong?	Pork stew, or beef, Mánong?
Lito:	Báka, Áding.	Beef, Áding.
Weytres:	Ania ti kayatyo nga inumen, Mánong?	What do you want to drink, Mánong?
Lito:	Kayatko ti 'coke.'	I want Coke.
Jesus:	Kayatko ti 'pepsi.'	I want Pepsi.
Oscar:	Kayatko ti kape.	I want coffee.
Manuel:	Kayatko ti gátas.	I want milk.
Reynaldo:	Danom láeng ti kayatko.	Water is all I want.
Weytres:	Ay, agúraykayo bassit! Saankayo nga aggigiddan. Sinno ti mayat ti danom?	Oh, wait a minute. Don't speak all at once. Who wants water?

Reynaldo:	Siak ti mayat ti danom.	I'm the one who wants water.
Weytres:	Sinno ti mayat ti 'coke'?	Who wants Coke?
Lito:	Siak ti mayat ti 'coke.'	I'm the one who wants Coke.
Weytres:	Sinno ti mayat ti 'pepsi'?	Who wants Pepsi?
Jesus:	Siak ti mayat ti 'pepsi.'	I'm the one who wants Pepsi.
Weytres:	Ket dakayo, Mánong?	And what about you, Mánong?
Oscar:	Kayatko ti kape. Daytoy kaduak, kayatna ti gátas.	I want coffee. This companion of mine, he wants milk.
	(Kalpasan ti trainta minútos)	(After thirty minutes)
Lito:	Ápo, nagbayag metten daydiay nga weytres!	Gee, what a long time that waitress is taking!
Jesus:	Ayanna, aya?	Where is she, I wonder?
Oscar:	Adda idiay uneg.	She's inside.
Manuel:	Ania ngata ti ar-aramídenna idiay?	What do you think she's doing in there?
Lito:	Hm. Diak ammo man!	Hm, I don't know!
Jesus:	Inka man kitáen no ápay a nakabaybayag.	Go and see why she's taking so long.
Reynaldo:	Ne, umáyen.	Look, she's coming now.
Lito:	Sssst. Ayan ti ordermi?	Sssst. Where's our order?
Weytres:	Lutlutuenda pay láeng, Mánong.	They're still cooking it, Mánong.
Lito:	Ay, santísima!	Oh, Holy Saints!
	(kalpasan ti baintesingko pay a minútos)	(After twenty-five minutes)
Lito:	Ania ti órasen, aya?	What's the time, now?
Reynaldo:	Ala únan.	It's already one o'clock.
Jesus:	Nganngáni maysa nga órastayo ditóyen.	We've been here nearly one hour already.
Manuel:	Ni, umay ti ordertayon!	Look, our order is coming now!
Oscar:	Ay, ápo, immay met láeng. Mabisinakon.	Oh, finally it has come! I'm hungry.
Weytres:	Dispensárenyo Mánong, ngem awan ti adóbo ken pinakbet ita. Kayatyo ti	Sorry, Mánong, but there isn't any *adóbo* or *pinakbet* today. Would

	agorder ti sabáli?	you like to order something different?
All:	Ay, ápay dímo imbaga itay? Ay, santísima! Intayon!	Oh, why didn't you tell us before? Holy Saints! Let's go!
Oscar:	Sigúro, baro a weytres.	Maybe she's a new waitress.
Jesus:	Sigúro, namúno a weytres.	Maybe she's a dumb waitress.
Reynaldo:	Ay, díka man agsásao ti kasta! Dákes dayta.	Hey, don't say that! That's terrible.

B. 'Tumáwarak Man, Nána?'
'May I Bargain, Nána?'

Irma:	Sagmamano dagitoy santol-yo, Nána?	How much are these *santols* of yours, Nána?
Nána:	Sagpipiséta, Nakkong.	Twenty centavos each, my child.
Irma:	Mabalin ti tumáwar, Nána?	Is it alright to bargain, Nána?
Nána:	Mabalin, Nakkong, ngem bassit láeng.	You can, my child, but only a little.
Irma:	Di pay la sagsisingko, Nána?	Couldn't it be five centavos each, Nána?
Nána:	Ay, saan, Nakkong! Nangína ti santol ita. Saan pay a puúnan dayta.	Oh, no, my child. *Santols* are expensive now. That wouldn't even cover the cost.
Irma:	Di pay la sagdidies, Nána?	Couldn't it be ten centavos each, Nána?
Nána:	Ay, saan, Balásangko. Saan a mabalin. Itedko kenka iti dua ti binting.	Oh, no, my young lady. It cannot be. I'll give you two for twenty-five centavos.
Irma:	Ala ngarod, Nána. Mabalin ti pumíli?	Okay, Nána. Is it all right to choose?
Nána:	Mabalin, ngem siak ti pumíli, a?	It's all right, but I'll be the one to choose, eh?
Irma:	Ala wen, Nána. Dagita dadakkel ken napipintas ti pilienyo, a?	Okay, Nána. Those big, nice looking ones are the ones you'll choose, huh?
Nána:	Ania ket daytoy balasángkon!	Oh, this girl! (Literally: Oh, this daughter of mine!)

C. 'Kasano ti Mapan Idiay . . . ?'
   'How to go to . . . ?'

Romy: Di la mabalin ti agsaludsod, Táta?

May I ask a question, Táta?

Táta: Mabalin, Barok. Ania ti kayatmo a saludsúden?

Alright, my young man. What do you want to ask?

Romy: Ammóyo ti ayan ti balay da Mr. Toribio ditoy, Táta?

Do you know where the house of Mr. Toribio is here, Táta?

Táta: Ay, adda idiay asideg ti simbáan.

Oh, it's there beside the church.

Romy: Kasano ti mapan idiay, Táta?

How does one get there, Táta?

Táta: Surútem daytoy a dálan aginggánat' makítam ti dakkel a pasdek a puraw. Labsam daydiay. Magnáka pay aginggánat' madánonmo ti Abenida Kaniógan. Agpakannawanka idiay, sáka agpakannigid iti sumaruno a kalsáda a Lucas Street. Surútem daydiay a kalsáda inggánat' makítam ti dakkel a simbáan ti Katóliko. Adda iti likudan ti simbáan ti balayda.

Follow this road until you see a big white building. Pass that. Keep on walking until you reach Kaniógan Avenue. Turn right there, then turn left on the following street which is Lucas Street. Follow that street until you see the large Catholic Church. Their home is behind the church.

Romy: Ania ti kolor ti balayda, Táta?

What is the color of their house, Táta?

Táta: Berde ken puraw, Barok. Adda áladna nga alambre.

Green and white, my young man. It has a wire

Romy: Malagipyo no ania ti nómerona, Táta?

Do you remember its number, Táta?

Táta: Ay, saan, Barok!

Oh, no, my young man!

Romy: Dios ti agngína, Táta. Kastá pay.

Thank you, Táta. Goodbye.

Táta: Kastá pay, Barok. No mayaw-awanka, agsaludsodka latta idiay. Ngem sápay koma ta díka mayaw-awan.

Goodbye, my young man. If you get lost just ask over there. But I hope you don't get lost.

D. 'Dimmagas ni Miding'
   'Miding Dropped By'

Miding: Ápo, addákayo? — Ápo, are you there?

Ápong Berta: Dumánonka, Nakkong. — Come in, my child.

Miding: Adda ni Carmen, Nána? — Is Carmen here, Nána?

Ápong Berta: Agúrayka bassit ta innak ayaban . . . Carmen, umayka man ta adda ni Miding! — Wait a little while I go call her . . . Carmen, would you come here because Miding is here?

Carmen: Agúraykayo bassit ta agsuksukátak. — Wait a minute, I'm changing.

Ápong Berta: Darsem ta agur-úray daytoy gayyemmo. Umayka mangan, Miding. — Hurry because your friend is waiting. Come and eat, Miding.

Miding: Saánen, Nana, ta nabsúgak pay. Kapangpanganko pay láeng idiay balay. — No, Nána, because I'm still full. I just ate at home.

Ápong Berta: Manganka úray no bassit láeng. — You eat, even a little.

Miding: Saának a mabisin, Nána. Dios ti agngína. — I'm not hungry, Nána, thank you.

Ápong Berta: Ay, díka man agbábain! Ne, addaytoy ti pingganmo. — Oh, don't be shy! Here is your plate.

Miding: Bassit láeng, Nána, ta nabsúgak pay. — Just a little, Nána, because I'm still full.

Ápong Berta: Ne, mangálaka ti sida. Addaytoy ti innapoy. Ne! — Here, get some meat. Here's the rice. Here!

Miding: Ala wen, Nána. — Okay, Nána.

Carmen: Intan, Miding. — Let's go now, Miding.

Ápong Berta: Agúrayka bassit ta mangmangan pay. Ne, mangálaka, pay. — Wait a minute, she's still eating. Here, have some more.

Miding: Huston, Nána. Bumtak ti buksitkon. — That's enough, Nána. My stomach's about to burst already.

Ápong Berta: Hm, nagbassit ti kinnanmo! Saanka a mabain ditoy balaymi. Ipabpabalaymo latta ditoy. — Hm, you ate so little! Don't be shy here in our house. Just feel at home here.

291

Miding:	Dios ti agngína, Nána. Inkamin.	Thank you, Nána. We're going now.
Ápong Berta:	Ala wen, Balásangko. Awan aniámanna. Dios ti kumúyog kadakayo.	Okay, my young lady. Don't mention it. God go with you.
Miding:	Dios ti agbáti, Nána.	God stay with you, Nána.

E. 'Nadúmadúma a Prútas'
  'Various Fruits'

John:	Ania dayta, Nána?	What's that, Nána?
Nána Osang:	Mangga, Nakkong.	It's a mango, my child.
John:	Nasam-it dayta?	Is it sweet?
Nána Osang:	Saan, saan a nasam-it. Naalsem dayta ta naáta. Naáta no berde.	No, it's not sweet. That one's sour because it's unripe. It's unripe if it's green.
John:	Ket no naluom, nasam-it?	What if it's ripe, is it sweet?
Nána Osang:	Wen, nasam-it.	Yes, it's sweet.
John:	Ania ti kolorna no naluom? Nalabbága?	What color is it if it's ripe? Is it red?
Nána Osang:	Saan, amarilio.	No, it's yellow.
John:	Saan a napait?	Isn't it bitter?
Nána Osang:	Saan, saan a napait.	No, it's not bitter.
John:	Ania met dayta, Nána?	And what's that, Nána?
Nána Osang:	Prútas met daytoy.	This is also fruit.
John:	Ania a prútas dayta?	What fruit is that?
Nána Osang:	Átis daytoy, Barok.	This is *átis,* my young man.
John:	Ket dagita, Nána. Ania dagita?	What about those, Nána, what are those?
Nána Osang:	Kaymíto dagitoy, Nakkong.	These are *kaymítos,* my child.
John:	Apo, nagpipintásen! Mangálaak man ti maysa a kaymíto, Nána? Ramanak man bassit.	Wow, how good they look! May I take one *kaymíto,* Nána? I'll taste it, if I may.

Nána Osang:	Ala wen, mangálaka latta. Mangálaka ti dua. Mangálaka met ti átis.	Yes, of course, just get some. Take two. Get some *átis,* too.
John:	Apo, nagsam-it! Nagímas! Ania ti nasamsam-it no naluom, Nána, daytoy kaymíto wenno dayta manga?	Wow, how sweet it is! How delicious it is! Which is sweeter when it's ripe, Nána, this *kaymíto,* or that mango?
Nána Osang:	Ay, nasamsam-it dayta mangga.	Oh, the mango is sweeter.
John:	Ania ti átis iti Inggles, Nána?	What is *átis* in English, Nána?
Nána Osang:	Diak ammo, Nakkong. Diak únay ammo ti aginggles. Ket sika, ápay ammom ti agilokano?	I don't know, my child. I really don't know how to speak English. What about you, how come you know how to speak Ilokano?
John:	Insúronak ni Mila, Nána.	Mila taught me, Nána.
Nána Osang:	Ay, nagsayáaten!	Oh, how nice!
John:	Ania ti kasam-ítan kadagitoy a prútas, Nána?	What is the sweetest among these fruits, Nána?
Nána Osang:	Nasam-itda ámin no naluomda.	They are all sweet when they're ripe.
John:	Naalsem met ti átis ken kaymíto no naáta, Nána?	Are *átis* and *kaymíto* sour when they're unripe, Nána?
Nána Osang:	Saan, nasugpetda no naáta.	No, they leave a furry feeling in your mouth when they're unripe.
John:	Saan a mabalin a kanen ti kaymíto no naata?	You can't eat *kaymítos* when they're unripe?
Nána Osang:	Ay, saan, Nakkong. Madi ti ramanna.	Oh, no, my child! They taste awful.
John:	Ket ti mangga, ngay.	What about mangoes?
Nána Osang:	Samman.	Yeah, you can.

Index To Grammar Notes

ONE

1. Predicate and subject
2. Genitive
3. KO set pronouns

TWO

1. AK set pronouns
2. *Ag-, mang-, -um-* verbs, *taga-* nouns, *na-* adjectives
3. Location phrase
4. Questions
   a. Yes-No
   b. Information
5. Locative gerunds

THREE

1. Reciprocal verbs, kinship terms
2. Plural determiners
3. *Ka--an* nouns
4. Non-kin-relationship terms
5. Negatives
6. Linkers

FOUR

1. SIAK set pronouns
2. Inclusive, exclusive and dual pronouns
3. Negative questions
4. Borrowings from Spanish
5. Sentence modifiers:
   a. *met*
   b. *gáyam*

FIVE

1. Locative determiner
2. Modified question words
3. Telling time
4. Sentence modifier: *-en*
5. Pseudo-verb: *kayat*

SIX

1. CVC- reduplication
   a. continuative
   b. customary
2. Direction auxiliary verbs
   a. *mapan, in-*
   b. *umay*
3. *Ápay* questions
4. Conjunctions: *ket* and *ken*
5. Time adverbs
6. Time phrases

SEVEN

1. Demonstratives
2. Patient-focus verbs: *-en*
3. Embedded sentences
4. Future tense
5. Compound predicates

EIGHT

1. Negative auxiliary verb: *di*
2. Patient-focus verbs: *-an*
3. Verb changes with *-um-*
4. Sentence modifiers
   a. *láeng*
   b. *man*
   c. *pay*
5. Adjectives
6. CVC- reduplication on patient-focus verbs

NINE

1. Past tense verb forms
   a. *ag-, mang-,* and *ma-*
   b. *-um-*
   c. *-en* and *-an*
   d. *pag--an*
2. Intensive adjectives

TEN

1. Patient-focus verbs: *i-*
2. Personal locative determiners
3. Auxiliary: *sa*
4. Idiom: *iso met la nga iso*

296

ELEVEN

1. Patient-focus verbs: deliberate vs. involuntary
2. Verb changes with *ma-*
3. Conjunction: *ta*
4. *kuna* say

TWELVE

1. Locative existentials: definite
2. Locative existentials: indefinite
3. Demonstrative determiners

THIRTEEN

1. Comparative adjectives
2. Plurals of nouns
3. Reason sentence: *ngamin*
4. Idiom: *saan a báli*
5. *dengngeg* listen, hear

FOURTEEN

1. Superlative adjectives
2. Plural of adjectives
3. Time gerunds

FIFTEEN

1. Possessive existentials

Production Notes

This book was designed by Roger Eggers.
Composition and paging were done on the
Quadex Composing System and typesetting on
the Compugraphic 8400 by the design and production staff of University of Hawaii Press.

The text and display typeface is Compugraphic
Times Roman.

Offset presswork and binding were done by
Malloy Lithographing, Inc. Text paper is Glat-
felter Offset Vellum, basis 50.